PRAYER JOURNAL FOR THE GROWING CHRISTIAN

One Day More Than We Deserve

Prayer Journal for the Growing Christian

Prayer Journal for the Growing Christian

One Day More Than We Deserve

Prayer Journal for the Growing Christian

Minister Onedia N. Gage, Ph. D.

PRAYER JOURNAL FOR THE GROWING CHRISTIAN

Other Books By
Minister Onedia N. Gage, Ph. D.

Are You Ready for 9th Grade . . . Again? A Family's Guide to Success
As We Grow Together Daily Devotional for Expectant Couples
As We Grow Together Prayer Journal for Expectant Couples
As We Grow Together: Workbook for Expectant Couples Her Workbook
As We Grow Together: Workbook for Expectant Couples His Workbook
The Best 40 Days of Your Life: A Journey of Spiritual Renewal
The Blue Print: Poetry for the Soul
From Fat to Fit in 90 Days: A Fitness Journal
From Two to One: The Notebook for the Christian Couple
Hannah's Voice: Powerful Lessons in Prayer
Her Story: The Legacy of Her Fight The Devotional
Her Story: The Legacy of Her Fight The Legacy Journal
Her Story: The Legacy of Her Fight Prayers and Journal
ILY! A Mother Daughter Relationship Workbook
In Her Own Words: Notebook for the Christian Woman
In Purple Ink: Poetry for the Spirit
The Intensive Retreat for Couples for Her
The Intensive Retreat for Couples for Him
Living a Whole Life: Sermons which Promote, Prompt and Provoke Life
Love Letters to God from a Teenage Girl
The Measure of a Woman: The Details of Her Soul
The Notebook: For Me, About Me, By Me
The Notebook for the Christian Teen
On This Journey Daily Devotional for Young People
On This Journey Prayer Journal for Young People
On This Journey Prayer Journal for Young People, Volume 2
One Day More Than We Deserve Prayer Journal for the Growing Christian
Promises, Promises: A Christian Novel
Queen in the Making: Bible Study for Teen Girls
Six Months of Solitude: The Sanctity of Singleness Notebook
Tools for These Times: Timely Sermons for Uncertain Times
With An Anointed Voice: The Power of Prayer
Yielded and Submitted: A Woman's Journey for a Life Dedicated to God
Yielded and Submitted: A Woman's Journey for a Life Dedicated to God Intimate Study
Yielded and Submitted: A Woman's Journey for a Life Dedicated to God Prayers and Journal

PRAYER JOURNAL FOR THE GROWING CHRISTIAN

Library of Congress

One Day More Than We Deserve
Prayer Journal for a Growing Christian

All Rights Reserved © 2012, 2017
Minister Onedia N. Gage, Ph. D.

No part of this of book may be reproduced or transmitted in
Any form or by any means, graphic, electronic, or mechanical,
Including photocopying, recording, taping, or by any
Information storage or retrieval system, without the
Permission in writing from the publisher.

Purple Ink, Inc. Press

For Information address:
Purple Ink, Inc.
P O Box 300113
Houston, TX 77230

www.purpleink.net ♦ onediagage@purpleink.net
www.onediagage.com ♦ onediagage@onediagage.com

ISBN:

978-1-939119-11-7

Printed in United States

The Word

1 Corinthians 3:6 (NIV)

⁶ I planted the seed, Apollos watered it, but God has been making it grow.

2 Peter 3:18 (NIV)

¹⁸ But grow in the grace and knowledge of our Lord and Savior Jesus Christ. To him be glory both now and forever! Amen.

Acts 16:5 (NIV)

⁵ So the churches were strengthened in the faith and grew daily in numbers.

The Dedication

To God, My Father

Thank You for constantly reminding me that everyday is designed for You

And one day more than I deserve.

To my children, Hillary and Nehemiah

May these words bless, drive, and inspire you to be the

Excellent servant God called each of us to be.

To my fellow servants

May these words call you forward out of shame, guilt, complacency, and any

other "STUFF" which prohibits us from serving God with our whole Heart.

One Day More Than We Deserve

Dear God,

Everyday is one day more than I deserve. I understand that. God, thank You for gifting me to author the books that I do. Father, thank You for loving me, forgiving me, and caring for me.

God, thank You for this daily devotional and prayer journal. I am eternally grateful that You gifted me and allowed me to deliver Your word—in both written and spoken format.

Thank You for everyday. Thank You for everyday that Your word does not return void through my life and ministry.

Thank You for allowing us to appreciate Your work and Creation.

Lord, I am working to use Your days better. Please forgive me for all previous misuse of Your days. Lord, I respect Your assignments and I will do everyday what I am called to do move closer to Your image. Thank You again for loving me and showing me to love others in that same profound and authentic manner.

Thank You for Jesus and thank You, Jesus!

Love Your Servant,
Onedia N. Gage

Dear Co-Laborer:

As you turn the pages of this journal and daily devotional, please know that I have prayed for You. This title alone indicates that we are learning to be more appreciative of God and more intentional about serving God. As we recognize that the days we have are more than we deserve and that we do not serve Him all the days well, we need to consider why we are here. We are here to serve God. Each additional day we have is one more than we deserve.

If God graded me when I disobeyed Him, acted unkind to others, and dismissed His voice, I would already been out of days. 14,000 days ago! <u>One Day More</u> reminds us of what is important to God.

Please use this devotional and journal prayerfully, considering all that God will reveal through these pages.

The twelve topics are God, Jesus, The Holy Spirit, Love, Prayer, Salvation, Praise & Worship, Wisdom, Heart, Service, Teaching, and Discipleship. As we examine each of these subjects, we will consider how to move closer to God. Each of these matters to God. He is missing parts of us. These are essential subjects where He wants all of us.

PRAYER JOURNAL FOR THE GROWING CHRISTIAN

<ins>One Day More</ins> is designed to share more of God with us. Read. Study. Meditate. Pray.

<ins>One Day More Than We Deserve</ins> drives us to God in an intimate fashion, to grow up and closer to God.

May this journal and devotional bless you!

Your Co-Laborer,

Onedia N. Gage

Minister Onedia N. Gage, Ph. D.

A Kinship With God

By Minister Onedia N. Gage, Ph. D.

Created me from dust
Formed me in her womb
Knew me
Know me
Plans for me

Disciple me
Discipline me
Gifted me
Equipped to serve You

Our love
Our friendship
My disobedience
Your forgiveness

A special communication
. . . prayer
A special encounter
. . . mediation
A special assignment
. . . gifts
A special relationship
. . . a friendship

A relationship where He speaks to me
Where my spirit communes with His
When You consider me
How You hear me

PRAYER JOURNAL FOR THE GROWING CHRISTIAN

This relationship
      This kinship nurtures my soul
      This kinship captures my spirit
      This kinship ministers to my hurts

The kinship is my life's love

The kinship of God—my refuge.

Reprinted from *In Purple Ink: Poetry for the Spirit*

Devotional & Journal Instructions

This is not your usual devotional, nor will the prayer journal be status quo. The devotional is designed to help us understand that each day that we have is one day more than we deserve.

Read the scripture for the day. Pray for an understanding of what you have read and pray for an opening to apply that scripture to your life. Read the commentary. Pray to understand how to likewise apply that commentary to your life.

Seek to share the lessons with others on this day. Pray continually throughout the day for the clarity you need and the audience God desires for you to serve Him best.

Table of Contents

The Word
The Dedication
The Letter to God
The Letter to the Reader
Poem: "A Kinship With God"
Devotional Instructions

God	25
Jesus	59
Holy Spirit	91
Salvation & Faith	125
Love	157
Prayer	191
Heart	223
Praise & Worship	257
Forgiveness	291
Teaching	323
Discipleship	357
Wisdom	389

Resources
Acknowledgements
Biography

The Prayer Journal

PRAYER JOURNAL FOR THE GROWING CHRISTIAN

God

There are many words which describe God given to us by Him. However we dare not define God with our finite subjectivity. As I consider the sovereignty of God, it becomes imperative that we grow closer to God in all that we do and with the incompleteness of who we are. We are His children! We are the result of the work of His Hands.

God loves us. God loves us enough for us to grow up and grow closer to Him. God loves us greatly. The greatness of His love has the power to move us away from sin. The sin that separates us and so easily entangles us is the element which needs to be eliminated.

God is omnipresent. He is ever-present, even in trouble, especially when we do not think He's there and even when we have moved away from Him. He is everywhere. Genesis 1:2b reads: "The Spirit of God was hovering over the waters." The expanse of the Spirit's reach is immeasurable, so I am unable to say how large the Spirit is in regard to how much water over which the Spirit hovered. I am comfortable with stating the water was incomplete in comparison to the Spirit. With that type of expanse and reach, He can certainly oversee my temporary setbacks and technical difficulties.

God, above all, is my God, my only God. Almighty God, the God that loves me unconditionally! God loves me when I hate myself! So He certainly loves me when I feel good about myself. God desires several things for us. We are to love Him, obey Him, share our gifts for this building of His kingdom, praise and worship Him, keep His commands, and work within the will of God.

God created me and He wants me to grow. My growth produces fruit. John 15:1 (NASB) reads "I am the true vine and My Father is the Vinedresser." God gives life to each us and He expects us to produce fruit in this life. God equips us for the work He designed us to do.

God is on each of these pages of this devotional and prayer journal. He is represented in your words and mine. God just wants ALL of you! ALL of us! God does not owe us anything. God has made us promises—ALL of which He will fulfill.

God is all powerful, all knowing, all loving, all forgiving, all encompassing, and all providing.

God. Grow in His presence because of His provision.

God.

January 1

Genesis 1:1 (NIV)

The Beginning

[1] In the beginning God created the heavens and the earth.

___

Thank You for thinking of me in the beginning.

January 2

Genesis 1:26-27 (NIV)

²⁶ Then God said, "Let us make mankind in our image, in our likeness, so that they may rule over the fish in the sea and the birds in the sky, over the livestock and all the wild animals, and over all the creatures that move along the ground."

²⁷ So God created mankind in his own image, in the image of God he created them; male and female he created them.

Lord, help me to represent You well at all times.

January 3

Genesis 6:3 (NIV)

³ Then the LORD said, "My Spirit will not contend with humans forever, for they are mortal; their days will be a hundred and twenty years."

_____

Lord, I apologize that I have disappointed You so much.

January 4

Genesis 6:5-7 (NIV)

⁵ The LORD saw how great the wickedness of the human race had become on the earth, and that every inclination of the thoughts of the human heart was only evil all the time. ⁶ The LORD regretted that he had made human beings on the earth, and his heart was deeply troubled. ⁷ So the LORD said, "I will wipe from the face of the earth the human race I have created—and with them the animals, the birds and the creatures that move along the ground—for I regret that I have made them."

_____
_____
_____
_____
_____
_____
_____
_____
_____
_____
_____
_____
_____
_____
_____

Lord, I never want You to be this angry ever again.

January 5

Deuteronomy 7:7-10 (MSG)

⁷⁻¹⁰ GOD wasn't attracted to you and didn't choose you because you were big and important—the fact is, there was almost nothing to you. He did it out of sheer love, keeping the promise He made to your ancestors. GOD stepped in and mightily bought you back out of that world of slavery, freed you from the iron grip of Pharaoh king of Egypt. Know this: GOD, your God, is God indeed, a God you can depend upon. He keeps His covenant of loyal love with those who love Him and observe His commandments for a thousand generations. But He also pays back those who hate Him, pays them the wages of death; He isn't slow to pay them off—those who hate Him, He pays right on time.

Thank You for Your 'sheer love' for me. I am grateful.

January 6

Genesis 2:21-22 (NIV)

²¹ So the LORD God caused the man to fall into a deep sleep; and while he was sleeping, he took one of the man's ribs and then closed up the place with flesh. ²² Then the LORD God made a woman from the rib he had taken out of the man, and he brought her to the man.

_____
_____
_____
_____
_____
_____
_____
_____
_____
_____
_____
_____
_____
_____
_____
_____
_____
_____
_____

Thank You for creating us, man and woman.

January 7

Genesis 12:1-3 (NIV)

The Call of Abram

¹ The LORD had said to Abram, "Go from your country, your people and your father's household to the land I will show you.
² "I will make you into a great nation,
and I will bless you;
I will make your name great,
and you will be a blessing.
³ I will bless those who bless you,
and whoever curses you I will curse;
and all peoples on earth
will be blessed through you."

Lord, thank You for Your awesome promises.

January 8

Genesis 22:1-2 (NIV)

Abraham Tested

[1] Some time later God tested Abraham. He said to him, "Abraham!" "Here I am," he replied.

[2] Then God said, "Take your son, your only son, whom you love—Isaac—and go to the region of Moriah. Sacrifice him there as a burnt offering on a mountain I will show you."

Lord, I await Your call to serve You and Your will.

January 9

Genesis 21:19 (NIV)

¹⁹ Then God opened her eyes and she saw a well of water. So she went and filled the skin with water and gave the boy a drink.

Lord, thank You for letting me see Your hand in my life.

PRAYER JOURNAL FOR THE GROWING CHRISTIAN

January 10

Exodus 20:1-17 (NIV)

The Ten Commandments

¹ And God spoke all these words:

² "I am the LORD your God, who brought you out of Egypt, out of the land of slavery.

³ "You shall have no other gods before[a] me.

⁴ "You shall not make for yourself an image in the form of anything in heaven above or on the earth beneath or in the waters below. ⁵ You shall not bow down to them or worship them; for I, the LORD your God, am a jealous God, punishing the children for the sin of the parents to the third and fourth generation of those who hate me, ⁶ but showing love to a thousand generations of those who love me and keep my commandments.

⁷ "You shall not misuse the name of the LORD your God, for the LORD will not hold anyone guiltless who misuses his name.

⁸ "Remember the Sabbath day by keeping it holy. ⁹ Six days you shall labor and do all your work, ¹⁰ but the seventh day is a sabbath to the LORD your God. On it you shall not do any work, neither you, nor your son or daughter, nor your male or female servant, nor your animals, nor any foreigner residing in your towns. ¹¹ For in six days the LORD made the heavens and the earth, the sea, and all that is in them, but he rested on the seventh day. Therefore the LORD blessed the Sabbath day and made it holy.

¹² "Honor your father and your mother, so that you may live long in the land the LORD your God is giving you.

¹³ "You shall not murder.

¹⁴ "You shall not commit adultery.

¹⁵ "You shall not steal.

¹⁶ "You shall not give false testimony against your neighbor.

¹⁷ "You shall not covet your neighbor's house. You shall not covet your neighbor's wife, or his male or female servant, his ox or donkey, or anything that belongs to your neighbor."

ONE DAY MORE THAN WE DESERVE

Lord, if only I could follow Your rules better. You made them so plain.

January 11

Exodus 34:1 (NIV)

The New Stone Tablets

¹ The LORD said to Moses, "Chisel out two stone tablets like the first ones, and I will write on them the words that were on the first tablets, which you broke.

Lord, thank You for second chances that we don't deserve.

January 12

Exodus 34:6-7 (NIV)

⁶ And he passed in front of Moses, proclaiming, "The LORD, the LORD, the compassionate and gracious God, slow to anger, abounding in love and faithfulness, ⁷ maintaining love to thousands, and forgiving wickedness, rebellion and sin. Yet he does not leave the guilty unpunished; he punishes the children and their children for the sin of the parents to the third and fourth generation."

Sovereign God, thank You for Your abounding love.

January 13

Leviticus 26:13 (NIV)

¹³ I am the LORD your God, who brought you out of Egypt so that you would no longer be slaves to the Egyptians; I broke the bars of your yoke and enabled you to walk with heads held high.

Father, thank You for breaking my chains . . . forever!

January 14

Deuteronomy 6:5 (NIV)

⁵ Love the LORD your God with all your heart and with all your soul and with all your strength.

Oh Lord, if I could only love You the way I am supposed to.

January 15

Deuteronomy 10:20 (NIV)

[20] Fear the LORD your God and serve him. Hold fast to him and take your oaths in his name.

Lord, thank You for creating areas for me to serve You.

January 16

Deuteronomy 32:4 (NIV)

⁴ He is the Rock, his works are perfect,
and all his ways are just.
A faithful God who does no wrong,
upright and just is he.

Thank You, Lord, for being faithful and just to me.

January 17

Isaiah 55:8-9 (NIV)

⁸ "For my thoughts are not your thoughts,
neither are your ways my ways,"
declares the LORD.
⁹ "As the heavens are higher than the earth,
so are my ways higher than your ways
and my thoughts than your thoughts.

Lord, thank goodness that Your thoughts are not my thoughts and Your ways are not my ways.

January 18

Psalm 46:10 (NIV)

¹⁰ He says, "Be still, and know that I am God;
I will be exalted among the nations,
I will be exalted in the earth."

___

Father, I will focus on being still. You are worth waiting on.

January 19

Joshua 1:5 (NIV)

⁵ No one will be able to stand against you all the days of your life. As I was with Moses, so I will be with you; I will never leave you nor forsake you.

Lord, thank You for being with me, especially when the people who were designed as support are a mirage.

January 20

Joshua 1:6 (NIV)

⁶ Be strong and courageous, because you will lead these people to inherit the land I swore to their ancestors to give them.

Thank You for strength and courage, Dear God, and thank You for the wisdom to use them when appropriate.

January 21

Joshua 1:9 (NIV)

⁹ Have I not commanded you? Be strong and courageous. Do not be afraid; do not be discouraged, for the LORD your God will be with you wherever you go."

_____
_____
_____
_____
_____
_____
_____
_____
_____
_____
_____
_____
_____
_____
_____
_____
_____
_____
_____

Thank You for covering me wherever I go, God Almighty.

January 22

1 Samuel 3:10 (NIV)

¹⁰ The LORD came and stood there, calling as at the other times, "Samuel! Samuel!" Then Samuel said, "Speak, for your servant is listening."

Father, Father, I am listening! Please talk to me!

PRAYER JOURNAL FOR THE GROWING CHRISTIAN

January 23

1 Samuel 16:1 (NIV)

Samuel Anoints David

The LORD said to Samuel, "How long will you mourn for Saul, since I have rejected him as king over Israel? Fill your horn with oil and be on your way; I am sending you to Jesse of Bethlehem. I have chosen one of his sons to be king."

_____
_____
_____
_____
_____
_____
_____
_____
_____
_____
_____
_____
_____
_____
_____

Lord, thank You for reminding me not to stay where You have delivered me from.

January 24

1 Samuel 16:12 (NIV)

¹² So he sent for him and had him brought in. He was glowing with health and had a fine appearance and handsome features.

Then the LORD said, "Rise and anoint him; this is the one."

Lord, thank You for choosing me based on my heart rather than my looks.

January 25

Psalm 51:10 (NIV)

[10] Create in me a pure heart, O God,
and renew a steadfast spirit within me.

_____
_____
_____
_____
_____
_____
_____
_____
_____
_____
_____
_____
_____
_____
_____
_____

Lord, if only I could keep the heart pure which You gave me, and thank You for restoring it back to Your desires.

January 26

Isaiah 52:7 (NIV)

⁷ How beautiful on the mountains
are the feet of those who bring good news,
who proclaim peace,
who bring good tidings,
who proclaim salvation,
who say to Zion,
"Your God reigns!"

Thank You, Lord for Your messengers. We need them.

PRAYER JOURNAL FOR THE GROWING CHRISTIAN

January 27

Jeremiah 31:33 (NIV)

[33] "This is the covenant I will make with the people of Israel after that time," declares the LORD.
"I will put my law in their minds
and write it on their hearts.
I will be their God,
and they will be my people.

Lord, thank You for choosing me and claiming me.

January 28

Jeremiah 32:27 (NIV)

27 "I am the LORD, the God of all mankind. Is anything too hard for me?

Lord, I am grateful that nothing is too hard for You.

January 29

Nahum 1:2 (NIV)

The LORD's Anger Against Nineveh

² The LORD is a jealous and avenging God;
the LORD takes vengeance and is filled with wrath.
The LORD takes vengeance on his foes
and vents his wrath against his enemies.

_____
_____
_____
_____
_____
_____
_____
_____
_____
_____
_____
_____
_____
_____
_____
_____
_____

God, I never want You that angry with me.

January 30

Genesis 2:7 (NIV)

⁷ Then the LORD God formed a man from the dust of the ground and breathed into his nostrils the breath of life, and the man became a living being.

Creator, thank You for creating me, my unworthy self.

January 31

2 Timothy 3:16 (NIV)

¹⁶ All Scripture is God-breathed and is useful for teaching, rebuking, correcting and training in righteousness,

---

Lord God, thank You for leaving us with The Instruction Manual. We need it!

ONE DAY MORE THAN WE DESERVE

Jesus Christ

When You are conceived by the Holy Spirit, knitted in the womb of a teenage virgin, and born in a manager outside in relatively cold weather, You are sure that You have a calling on Your life. Jesus Christ arrived on Earth in a special way. Jesus was methodically prepared for the ministry God had designed.

Jesus lived 33 years and His impact has lasted for over two thousand years and will last forevermore. Jesus was a teaching, preaching, prayer warrior. This Ministry also gives life to particular humans by raising them from the dead or healing them before a "premature" death. Likewise, this Ministry brought light and served notice to darkness that it was not welcomed and His followers are protected by His blood.

Jesus is our definition of love. He loves us completely and fully and without reservation. When we consider how He loves us and His command for us to love others, this is the ultimate love. A love we have difficulty translating to others and offering ourselves. Jesus demonstrates His love for us in so many methods and with such capacity that we can only comprehend His love in portions. He is so overwhelming as He loves us, we cannot possibly duplicate that love at His level. We must try to love at that level. We need to give effort—EXTREME! He loves us better than we will ever love ourselves and especially how we love others. The quality of that love likewise should reflect His care, concern and compassion.

His teaching is the best example of how to share knowledge. As a teacher, I use Jesus' methods to teach about Jesus. Jesus is direct in His teaching. He is thorough in His explanation. Jesus uses lots of parables to share the truth He is teaching. His approach is not always received immediately however, He is persistent in His methodology. Jesus teaches us from His study and His knowledge given by God and the Holy Spirit.

Jesus treats as His friend. He lived a sin-free life and experienced the temptations and betrayal that we all do. He is our example for perseverance. The knowledge that He shares is transparent and authentic. He is faithful to God's word. He earnestly seeks us and desires us to be saved and to know the truth. The Great Commission which He leaves with us, is His need for co-laborers. The need we have is to share in the work. We should be ecstatic to share in God's work to help others know Him and serve Him.

Jesus Christ came to save us from the sin that so easily entangles us. He loves us and wants us to love Him.

February 1

Matthew 1:16 (NIV 1984)

[16] and Jacob the father of Joseph, the husband of Mary, of whom was born Jesus, who is called Christ.

Thank You, Father, for Your Son, Jesus Christ.

February 2

Matthew 1:20-23 (NIV 1984)

[20] But after he had considered this, an angel of the Lord appeared to him in a dream and said, "Joseph son of David, do not be afraid to take Mary home as your wife, because what is conceived in her is from the Holy Spirit. [21] She will give birth to a son, and you are to give him the name Jesus, because he will save his people from their sins."

[22] All this took place to fulfill what the Lord had said through the prophet: [23] "The virgin will be with child and will give birth to a son, and they will call him Immanuel"—which means, "God with us."

_____
_____
_____
_____
_____
_____
_____
_____
_____
_____
_____
_____
_____
_____
_____
_____

Lord, what a beautiful legacy to gift us with: Your Son.

ONE DAY MORE THAN WE DESERVE

February 3

Luke 1:41-46 (NIV 1984)

⁴¹ When Elizabeth heard Mary's greeting, the baby leaped in her womb, and Elizabeth was filled with the Holy Spirit. ⁴² In a loud voice she exclaimed: "Blessed are you among women, and blessed is the child you will bear! ⁴³ But why am I so favored, that the mother of my Lord should come to me? ⁴⁴ As soon as the sound of your greeting reached my ears, the baby in my womb leaped for joy. ⁴⁵ Blessed is she who has believed that what the Lord has said to her will be accomplished!"

_____
_____
_____
_____
_____
_____
_____
_____
_____
_____
_____
_____
_____
_____
_____
_____

Lord, the Holy Spirit dwells within me and if I am attentive, He will leap within me as well. I'm attentive!

February 4

Luke 2:49-50 (NIV 1984)

⁴⁹ "Why were you searching for me?" he asked. "Didn't you know I had to be in my Father's house?" ⁵⁰ But they did not understand what he was saying to them.

Lord, thank You for Mary's example of a great Mom.

… ONE DAY MORE THAN WE DESERVE

February 5

Luke 3:21-22 (NIV 1984)

The Baptism and Genealogy of Jesus

[21] When all the people were being baptized, Jesus was baptized too. And as he was praying, heaven was opened [22] and the Holy Spirit descended on him in bodily form like a dove. And a voice came from heaven: "You are my Son, whom I love; with you I am well pleased."

Jesus, thank You for leading by example!

February 6

John 1:1-2 (NIV)

The Word Became Flesh

¹ In the beginning was the Word, and the Word was with God, and the Word was God. ² He was with God in the beginning.

Lord, You left Your Holy Word to walk among us! Amen!

February 7

John 4:34 (NIV)

34 "My food," said Jesus, "is to do the will of Him who sent me and to finish his work.

Jesus, if I only be motivated and focused the way You are to do the work of God, the One who sent us.

February 8

John 12:44-46 (NIV)

44 Then Jesus cried out, "Whoever believes in me does not believe in me only, but in the one who sent me. 45 The one who looks at me is seeing the one who sent me. 46 I have come into the world as a light, so that no one who believes in me should stay in darkness.

_____
_____
_____
_____
_____
_____
_____
_____
_____
_____
_____
_____
_____
_____
_____
_____
_____
_____

I believe in You, God, and Jesus Christ, Your Son, and the Holy Spirit, the Comforter You sent.

February 9

John 12:47 (NIV)

⁴⁷ "If anyone hears my words but does not keep them, I do not judge that person. For I did not come to judge the world, but to save the world.

Christ, thank You for saving me and not judging me. I am in need of saving; sometimes from my own self.

February 10

John 12:49 (NIV)

⁴⁹ For I did not speak on my own, but the Father who sent me commanded me to say all that I have spoken.

Jesus, thank You for Your obedience to do God's will and to teach God's messages. We appreciate Your example.

February 11

John 12:50 (NIV)

⁵⁰ I know that His command leads to eternal life. So whatever I say is just what the Father has told me to say."

I know that His word leads to eternal life and I still stray away. Jesus, please help.

February 12

John 14:23 (NIV)

²³ Jesus replied, "Anyone who loves me will obey my teaching. My Father will love them, and we will come to them and make our home with them.

Jesus, I am having trouble with the obey part. Please guide. Thank You!

One Day More Than We Deserve

February 13

John 14:27 (NIV)

²⁷ Peace I leave with you; My peace I give you. I do not give to you as the world gives. Do not let your hearts be troubled and do not be afraid.

___

Jesus, Your peace is so powerful. Thank You for teaching us to give what we possess to others since we did not create it ourselves.

Prayer Journal for the Growing Christian

February 14

John 15:1-2 (NIV)

The Vine and the Branches

¹ "I am the True Vine, and my Father is the Gardener. ² He cuts off every branch in Me that bears no fruit, while every branch that does bear fruit He prunes so that it will be even more fruitful.

_____
_____
_____
_____
_____
_____
_____
_____
_____
_____
_____
_____
_____
_____
_____
_____
_____
_____
_____
_____

Jesus, thank You for helping me bear fruit.

February 15

John 15:18-19 (NIV)

The World Hates the Disciples

¹⁸ "If the world hates you, keep in mind that it hated me first. ¹⁹ If you belonged to the world, it would love you as its own. As it is, you do not belong to the world, but I have chosen you out of the world. That is why the world hates you.

___

Christ, thank You for reminding me of what could happen for belonging to God.

February 16

John 15:21 (NIV)

[21] They will treat you this way because of my name, for they do not know the one who sent me.

Jesus, I do not like being treated this way. I know You disliked it more.

February 17

John 15:4 (NIV)

⁴ Remain in Me, as I also remain in you. No branch can bear fruit by itself; it must remain in the Vine. Neither can you bear fruit unless you remain in Me.

Jesus, thank You for defining how fruit is produced. I pray to be a producer of fruit.

PRAYER JOURNAL FOR THE GROWING CHRISTIAN

February 18

John 15:5 (NIV)

⁵ "I am the vine; you are the branches. If you remain in Me and I in you, you will bear much fruit; apart from Me you can do nothing.

_____
_____
_____
_____
_____
_____
_____
_____
_____
_____
_____
_____
_____
_____
_____
_____
_____

Jesus, thank You for teaching me how to be a great branch.

February 19

John 15:13 (NIV)

¹³ Greater love has no one than this: to lay down one's life for one's friends.

Jesus, help me to be able to love like that! I need to know.

February 20

Matthew 11:28-30 (NIV)

[28] "Come to me, all you who are weary and burdened, and I will give you rest. [29] Take my yoke upon you and learn from me, for I am gentle and humble in heart, and you will find rest for your souls. [30] For my yoke is easy and my burden is light."

_____
_____
_____
_____
_____
_____
_____
_____
_____
_____
_____
_____
_____
_____
_____
_____

Jesus, thank You for offering me a safe, no strings attached place to rest. I need You always.

February 21

John 12:7-8 (NIV)

[7] "Leave her alone," Jesus replied. "It was intended that she should save this perfume for the day of my burial. [8] You will always have the poor among you, but you will not always have me."

Jesus, thank You for helping me to keep my priorities in order.

February 22

John 11:35 (NIV)

[35] Jesus wept.

Jesus, I want the type of compassion You exhibit. Daily.

February 23

John 16:24 (NIV)

[24] Until now you have not asked for anything in my name. Ask and you will receive, and your joy will be complete.

___

Jesus, thank You for the gift of calling Your name in prayer. Amen!

February 24

Luke 23:34 (NIV)

[34] Jesus said, "Father, forgive them, for they do not know what they are doing." And they divided up his clothes by casting lots.

Jesus, I want to forgive like You. I have so much work to do.

February 25

Luke 23:42 (NIV)

[42] Then he said, "Jesus, remember me when you come into your kingdom."

_____
_____
_____
_____
_____
_____
_____
_____
_____
_____
_____
_____
_____
_____
_____
_____
_____
_____

Jesus, I know that this a big request, but please remember me.

PRAYER JOURNAL FOR THE GROWING CHRISTIAN

February 26

Luke 23:46 (NIV)

[46] Jesus called out with a loud voice, "Father, into your hands I commit my spirit." When he had said this, he breathed his last.

Jesus, Your total surrender to God causes me to hold my head down in shame. I'm working to surrender accordingly.

February 27

Matthew 28:9-10 (NIV)

⁹ Suddenly Jesus met them. "Greetings," he said. They came to him, clasped his feet and worshiped him. ¹⁰ Then Jesus said to them, "Do not be afraid. Go and tell my brothers to go to Galilee; there they will see me."

Thank You, Jesus, for reminding me not to be afraid.

February 28

Matthew 26:39 (NIV)

³⁹ Going a little farther, he fell with his face to the ground and prayed, "My Father, if it is possible, may this cup be taken from me. Yet not as I will, but as you will."

_____
_____
_____
_____
_____
_____
_____
_____
_____
_____
_____
_____
_____
_____
_____
_____
_____

Jesus, thank You for sharing the value of laying on my face before the Lord.

February 29

Mark 15:33-34 (NIV)

The Death of Jesus

³³ At noon, darkness came over the whole land until three in the afternoon. ³⁴ And at three in the afternoon Jesus cried out in a loud voice, *"Eloi, Eloi, lema sabachthani?"* (which means "My God, my God, why have you forsaken me?").

_____
_____
_____
_____
_____
_____
_____
_____
_____
_____
_____
_____
_____
_____
_____

Lord, I know that we could not have You forever but I still have questions and would have liked to have some time with You.

PRAYER JOURNAL FOR THE GROWING CHRISTIAN

The Holy Spirit

Jesus Christ told us that God would gift us with the Holy Spirit as an intercessor and an indweller of our spirits. The Holy Spirit is a communicator on God's and Jesus' behalf. The Holy Spirit has the power to pray for us when we do not know what to pray (Romans 8:26-27). The Spirit knows God's will for my life. Because of the Spirit's knowledge. It intercedes to God on my behalf; particularly when I do not what to pray for.

The Holy Spirit offers us His comfort. The comfort is based on what God and Jesus offers as a provision. This provision is God's hand as a reminder on our lives. We need to be mindful of His indwelling of us. The Holy Spirit considers our hearts as He dwells written us.

The Holy Spirit helps us address the Father, Our God. There are times when I cannot muster enough energy, or willpower to pray. I certainly do not always know what to say when I pray. For this reason the Holy Spirit acts as our intercessor.

The Holy Spirit insures that we remain close to God. John 14:15-18 reads, "[15] "If you love me, keep my commands. [16] And I will ask the Father, and he will give you another advocate to help you and be with you forever— [17] the Spirit of truth. The world cannot accept him, because it neither sees him nor knows him. But you know him, for he lives with you and will be in you.""

We are to live in the Spirit. Romans 8 sets the foundation for the life we are to lead. [9] You, however, are not in the realm of the flesh but are in the realm of the Spirit, if indeed the Spirit of God lives in you. And if anyone does not have the Spirit of Christ, they do not belong to Christ. [10] But if Christ is in you, then even though your body is subject to death because of sin, the Spirit gives life because of righteousness. [11] And if the Spirit of him who raised Jesus from the dead is living in you, he who raised Christ from the dead will also give life to your mortal bodies because of his Spirit who lives in you.

The Holy Spirit is the guiding force and the foundation for our lives. Stay close to the Holy Spirit! He is already close to you!

March 1

Matthew 1:18 (NIV)

Joseph Accepts Jesus as His Son

[18] This is how the birth of Jesus the Messiah came about: His mother Mary was pledged to be married to Joseph, but before they came together, she was found to be pregnant through the Holy Spirit.

_____
_____
_____
_____
_____
_____
_____
_____
_____
_____
_____
_____
_____
_____
_____
_____
_____

Thank You for Joseph's obedience. May he continue to serve as example to us all.

March 2

Matthew 3:11 (NIV)

¹¹ "I baptize you with water for repentance. But after me comes one who is more powerful than I, whose sandals I am not worthy to carry. He will baptize you with the Holy Spirit and fire.

_____
_____
_____
_____
_____
_____
_____
_____
_____
_____
_____
_____
_____
_____
_____
_____
_____

Thank You for the repentance of baptism.

March 3

Matthew 28:19 (NIV)

[19] Therefore go and make disciples of all nations, baptizing them in the name of the Father and of the Son and of the Holy Spirit,

Thank You, Jesus, for the power of Your assignment.

PRAYER JOURNAL FOR THE GROWING CHRISTIAN

March 4

Luke 11:13 (NIV)

[13] If you then, though you are evil, know how to give good gifts to your children, how much more will your Father in heaven give the Holy Spirit to those who ask Him!"

_____
_____
_____
_____
_____
_____
_____
_____
_____
_____
_____
_____
_____
_____
_____
_____
_____

Thank You for Your love and care and provision, Lord.

March 5

Luke 1:80 (NIV)

[80] And the Child grew and became strong in spirit; and He lived in the wilderness until He appeared publicly to Israel.

Jesus, thank You for the ability to be strong in spirit.

March 6

John 4:24 (NIV)

24 God is spirit, and His worshipers must worship in the Spirit and in truth."

Thank You God but we are often confused by the understanding of spirit and truth.

March 7

John 7:39 (NIV)

³⁹ By this He meant the Spirit, whom those who believed in Him were later to receive. Up to that time the Spirit had not been given, since Jesus had not yet been glorified.

I guess I cannot return the Spirit in trade of You, Jesus, so I am thankful for Your will, Lord.

March 8

John 14:26 (NIV)

²⁶ But the Advocate, the Holy Spirit, whom the Father will send in My name, will teach you all things and will remind you of everything I have said to you.

Jesus, thank You for the gift of the Holy Spirit.

March 9

John 16:13 (NIV)

[13] But when He, the Spirit of truth, comes, He will guide you into all the truth. He will not speak on His own; He will speak only what He hears, and He will tell you what is yet to come.

___

Jesus, thank You for leaving us with some help.

PRAYER JOURNAL FOR THE GROWING CHRISTIAN

March 10

John 20:22-23 (NIV)

[22] And with that He breathed on them and said, "Receive the Holy Spirit.

_____
_____
_____
_____
_____
_____
_____
_____
_____
_____
_____
_____
_____
_____
_____
_____
_____
_____
_____

Jesus, this Advocate that You have left us is a great gift and I appreciate Someone to help me with my needs.

March 11

Acts 2:4 (NIV)

⁴ All of them were filled with the Holy Spirit and began to speak in other tongues as the Spirit enabled them.

Thank You God, for the filling with the Holy Spirit.

March 12

Acts 2:38 (NIV)

[38] Peter replied, "Repent and be baptized, every one of you, in the name of Jesus Christ for the forgiveness of your sins. And you will receive the gift of the Holy Spirit.

Thank You for the teachings of Peter, God.

March 13

Acts 6:3 (NIV)

³ Brothers and sisters, choose seven men from among you who are known to be full of the Spirit and wisdom.

God, thank You for those You send around me with the Holy Spirit.

March 14

Acts 19:2 (NIV)

² and asked them, "Did you receive the Holy Spirit when you believed?" They answered, "No, we have not even heard that there is a Holy Spirit."

Thank You God, for teaching me about the Holy Spirit.

March 15

Romans 8:9 (NIV)

⁹ You, however, are not in the realm of the flesh but are in the realm of the Spirit, if indeed the Spirit of God lives in you. And if anyone does not have the Spirit of Christ, they do not belong to Christ.

Holy Spirit, thank You for dwelling within me and me belonging to You.

PRAYER JOURNAL FOR THE GROWING CHRISTIAN

March 16

Romans 8:26 (NIV)

[26] In the same way, the Spirit helps us in our weakness. We do not know what we ought to pray for, but the Spirit himself intercedes for us through wordless groans.

Holy Spirit, thank You for helping me in my weakness and praying when I can muster the words.

March 17

1 Corinthians 2:10 (NIV)

[10] these are the things God has revealed to us by his Spirit. The Spirit searches all things, even the deep things of God.

Holy Spirit, thank You for searching me and knowing me. Thank You for revealing things to me that only You can.

March 18

1 Corinthians 6:19 (NIV)

[19] Do you not know that your bodies are temples of the Holy Spirit, who is in you, whom you have received from God? You are not your own;

_____
_____
_____
_____
_____
_____
_____
_____
_____
_____
_____
_____
_____
_____
_____
_____

Holy Spirit, thank You for reminding me that I am not my own and that You live within me. I am sorry that I do not give You a great place to stay.

March 19

2 Corinthians 5:5 (NIV)

⁵ Now the one who has fashioned us for this very purpose is God, who has given us the Spirit as a deposit, guaranteeing what is to come.

_____

God, we are unworthy of all that You do and provide.

March 20

Galatians 5:16 (NIV)

¹⁶ So I say, walk by the Spirit, and you will not gratify the desires of the flesh.

_____
_____
_____
_____
_____
_____
_____
_____
_____
_____
_____
_____
_____
_____
_____
_____
_____

Where is the Spirit when I choose to leave Him to sin? Help me, Holy Spirit when I want to gratify the desires of the flesh.

March 21

Galatians 5:22 (NIV)

²² But the fruit of the Spirit is love, joy, peace, forbearance, kindness, goodness, faithfulness,

Thank You Holy Spirit, for producing the fruit within us so that we can live according to God's will.

March 22

Galatians 5:25 (NIV)

[25] Since we live by the Spirit, let us keep in step with the Spirit.

Help me to stay in step with You, Holy Spirit.

March 23

Ephesians 1:13 (NIV)

[13] And you also were included in Christ when you heard the message of truth, the gospel of your salvation. When you believed, you were marked in him with a seal, the promised Holy Spirit,

_____
_____
_____
_____
_____
_____
_____
_____
_____
_____
_____
_____
_____
_____
_____
_____
_____
_____
_____
_____

God, thank You for making it easy to be Your child.

March 24

Ephesians 4:30 (NIV)

³⁰ And do not grieve the Holy Spirit of God, with whom you were sealed for the day of redemption.

Lord, I pray to stop grieving the Holy Spirit; I do with no good reason.

March 25

Ephesians 6:17 (NIV)

[17] Take the helmet of salvation and the sword of the Spirit, which is the word of God.

Lord, thank You for the equipment which You provide for my protection and strength. It is a prayer answered.

March 26

Genesis 1:2 (NIV)

² Now the earth was formless and empty, darkness was over the surface of the deep, and the Spirit of God was hovering over the waters.

Lord, that image made me different; thank You for hovering over me!

March 27

2 Thessalonians 2:13 (NIV)

[13] But we ought always to thank God for you, brothers and sisters loved by the Lord, because God chose you as first fruits to be saved through the sanctifying work of the Spirit and through belief in the truth.

Thank You, for the work of the Spirit. It is what keeps me whole.

March 28

2 Peter 1:21 (NIV)

²¹ For prophecy never had its origin in the human will, but prophets, though human, spoke from God as they were carried along by the Holy Spirit.

Oh Lord to be trusted by You is what I yearn for!

March 29

Isaiah 63:10 (NIV)

¹⁰ Yet they rebelled
and grieved his Holy Spirit.
So he turned and became their enemy
and he himself fought against them.

Father, I pray to stop grieving the Holy Spirit.

PRAYER JOURNAL FOR THE GROWING CHRISTIAN

March 30

Job 33:4 (NIV)

⁴ The Spirit of God has made me;
the breath of the Almighty gives me life.

_____
_____
_____
_____
_____
_____
_____
_____
_____
_____
_____
_____
_____
_____
_____
_____
_____
_____

Lord, thank You for creating me and breathing Your life on me. Your breath is an investment in me. I am sorry that I disappoint You so very often.

March 31

Luke 23:46 (NIV)

⁴⁶ Jesus called out with a loud voice, "Father, into Your hands I commit my spirit." When He had said this, He breathed His last.

___

Lord, I commit my lowly spirit to You. Please raise it to something which represents You well.

Faith & Salvation

Faith is the evidence of what's hoped for but is yet unseen. Hebrews 11:1.

Faith is knowing that God is in control of the situation even though we "feel" alone. Faith is remembering that God is aware of everything that happens to us. He is aware of our circumstances in real time—not because we yelled out of pain to Him to rescue us from our circumstances. Faith is understanding that we are not the ones taking the risk on us—God risks His reputation based on how others perceive that we are faithful. Hebrews 11:6 MSG states it this way: "It's impossible to please God apart from faith. And why? Because anyone who wants to approach God must believe both that He exists and that He cares enough to respond to those who seek Him."

Faith is believing that God's plans are more comprehensive than the trouble that you have. Faith is knowing that God knows how much you can bear. Faith requires you to stretch beyond your imagination—your perception your boundaries.

Faith is the mechanism which keeps us from our "edge"—the place where we arrive when we feel we cannot withstand another event, circumstance, issue, death, loss or bad report. Faith is what drives us to our knees seeking God for His guidance, His peace, His love and His leadership.

Faith is what we share when we want to quit bur cannot because others are depending on your faith to make it through their storms.

Faith is believing God is an unwavering manner for all that He promised. Faith is understanding that what you ask, even if you ask in His name, if it does not match His will, you will not be granted. Faith is knowing that the best outcome will be selected for you, even though you may not agree. Faith is understanding that God believes and trusts you to do your best with what He's given you.

Faith binds us to God. Faith aligns us with God. When we have faith, we believe in God, His process, His methods, His timing and His plan. When we have genuine faith, we TRUST God—completely. We do TRUST God but sometimes on some limited terms, under specific circumstances and especially if we get our way, in our timing. That is not faith—that is how we behave with our friends and family, colleagues and enemies. Faith is taking God at His word. Faith is believing past available visual evidence. Faith is based on our hearts. Does He have our whole heart?

April 1

Psalm 27:1 (KJV)

¹ The LORD is my light and my salvation; whom shall I fear? the LORD is the strength of my life; of whom shall I be afraid?

_____
_____
_____
_____
_____
_____
_____
_____
_____
_____
_____
_____
_____
_____
_____
_____

Thank You God for being my light, my salvation, and my strength; I shall not be afraid!

April 2

Jonah 2:9 (KJV)

⁹ But I will sacrifice unto thee with the voice of thanksgiving; I will pay that that I have vowed. Salvation is of the LORD.

Lord, thank You for saving me, for Your salvation of my sorry, overwhelmed soul. I cry for You.

April 3

Ephesians 6:17 (NIV)

¹⁷ Take the helmet of salvation and the sword of the Spirit, which is the word of God.

Lord, the salvation which I take for granted, I need desperately. I love You, God. Thank You.

April 4

Acts 4:12 (NIV)

¹² Salvation is found in no one else, for there is no other name under heaven given to mankind by which we must be saved."

Lord, the salvation which You provide—it is freedom and it is hope. Help me share with others so that others can be made whole.

April 5

John 10:10 (NASB)

¹⁰ The thief comes only to steal and kill and destroy; I came that they may have life, and have *it* abundantly.

Lord, I am often confused about this abundance part—it is You, rather than things, You want us to have more of.

April 6

Romans 6:23 (KJV)

²³ For the wages of sin is death; but the gift of God is eternal life through Jesus Christ our Lord.

Lord, thank You for the provision of eternal life through the sacrifices of Christ.

April 7

Ephesians 2:8-10 (MSG)

⁷⁻¹⁰ Now God has us where He wants us, with all the time in this world and the next to shower grace and kindness upon us in Christ Jesus. Saving is all His idea, and all His work. All we do is trust Him enough to let Him do it. It's God's gift from start to finish! We don't play the major role. If we did, we'd probably go around bragging that we'd done the whole thing! No, we neither make nor save ourselves. God does both the making and saving. He creates each of us by Christ Jesus to join Him in the work He does, the good work He has gotten ready for us to do, work we had better be doing.

Lord, You are right I would take credit and I would pursue other things other than You.

April 8

Romans 3:23 (KJV)

[23] For all have sinned, and come short of the glory of God;

Lord, I wished I did not sin so easily.

April 9

John 3:16 (MSG)

16 "This is how much God loved the world: He gave his Son, His one and only Son. And this is why: so that no one need be destroyed; by believing in Him, anyone can have a whole and lasting life.

Thank You, God for Your unbelievable gift!

April 10

Deuteronomy 7:9 (NIV)

⁹ Know therefore that the LORD your God is God; He is the faithful God, keeping His covenant of love to a thousand generations of those who love him and keep His commandments.

Lord, thank You for the promise of Your provision.

April 11

Matthew 25:21 (NIV)

[21] "His master replied, 'Well done, good and faithful servant! You have been faithful with a few things; I will put you in charge of many things. Come and share your master's happiness!'

___

Lord, oh how I yearn to hear those words.

April 12

Hebrews 10:23 (KJV)

[23] Let us hold fast the profession of our faith without wavering; (for he is faithful that promised)

_____
_____
_____
_____
_____
_____
_____
_____
_____
_____
_____
_____
_____
_____
_____
_____
_____
_____
_____
_____

Lord, help me to remain faithful. Remind me when I am, that You should not have to remind me.

April 13

Matthew 9:29 (NASB)

[29] Then He touched their eyes, saying, "It shall be done to you according to your faith."

Lord, thank You for recognizing my faith.

PRAYER JOURNAL FOR THE GROWING CHRISTIAN

April 14

Matthew 17:20 (NIV)

[20] He replied, "Because you have so little faith. Truly I tell you, if you have faith as small as a mustard seed, you can say to this mountain, 'Move from here to there,' and it will move. Nothing will be impossible for you."

_____
_____
_____
_____
_____
_____
_____
_____
_____
_____
_____
_____
_____
_____
_____

Lord, help me to increase my faith. It seems so offensive that I have so little faith when You have shown multiple reasons why I should have more than just a mustard seed.

ONE DAY MORE THAN WE DESERVE

April 15

Mark 11:22 (NIV)

²² "Have faith in God," Jesus answered.

Jesus, thank You for reminding me to have faith in the God who created me and who deserves my undeniable faith, which often fails Him.

April 16

Luke 7:9 (NIV)

⁹ When Jesus heard this, He was amazed at him, and turning to the crowd following him, He said, "I tell you, I have not found such great faith even in Israel."

Thank You for recognizing the faith that I should have, Jesus.

April 17

Luke 12:28 (NIV)

[28] If that is how God clothes the grass of the field, which is here today, and tomorrow is thrown into the fire, how much more will he clothe you—you of little faith!

_____
_____
_____
_____
_____
_____
_____
_____
_____
_____
_____
_____
_____
_____
_____
_____
_____
_____
_____
_____

Lord, why do I have such little faith?

April 18

Romans 10:17 (NIV)

¹⁷ Consequently, faith comes from hearing the message, and the message is heard through the word about Christ.

Jesus, I am going to listen intently and intentionally more messages so that I can upgrade my faith.

April 19

2 Corinthians 5:7 (NKJV)

⁷ For we walk by faith, not by sight.

_____

Lord Jesus, help me walk by an unprecedented faith so that I can do what You created, prepared, and planned for me to do.

April 20

Ephesians 4:5 (KJV)

⁵ One Lord, one faith, one baptism,

Lord, I am your child and I hope that I can stop disappointing You.

April 21

Hebrews 11:1 (KJV)

¹ Now faith is the substance of things hoped for, the evidence of things not seen.

_____
_____
_____
_____
_____
_____
_____
_____
_____
_____
_____
_____
_____
_____
_____
_____
_____
_____

Lord, I so want to be the faithful so that You can be proud. I want to impress You with my faith. I'm not close.

April 22

Hebrews 11:6 (NIV)

⁶ And without faith it is impossible to please God, because anyone who comes to him must believe that he exists and that he rewards those who earnestly seek him.

_____
_____
_____
_____
_____
_____
_____
_____
_____
_____
_____
_____
_____
_____
_____
_____
_____
_____

Lord, I so want to please You!

April 23

Hebrews 12:2 (KJV)

² Looking unto Jesus the author and finisher of our faith; who for the joy that was set before him endured the cross, despising the shame, and is set down at the right hand of the throne of God.

___

Jesus, You are the author and finisher of my faith. You make me completely whole. You are to be followed forever.

April 24

Romans 1:12 (NIV)

¹² that is, that you and I may be mutually encouraged by each other's faith.

Jesus, thank You for sending me near people who can help enhance my faith. I hope that I can do the same for them.

April 25

James 2:14 (NIV)

Faith and Deeds

[14] What good is it, my brothers and sisters, if someone claims to have faith but has no deeds? Can such faith save them?

_____
_____
_____
_____
_____
_____
_____
_____
_____
_____
_____
_____
_____
_____
_____
_____
_____

Lord, I will work while I wait on the fulfillment of Your will.

April 26

Psalm 117:2 (NIV)

² For great is his love toward us,
and the faithfulness of the LORD endures forever.

Praise the LORD.

_____
_____
_____
_____
_____
_____
_____
_____
_____
_____
_____
_____
_____
_____
_____
_____
_____

Thank You, Lord, for the foreverness of Your love and faith.

April 27

Psalm 119:75 (NASB)

⁷⁵ I know, O LORD, that Your judgments are righteous,
And that in faithfulness You have afflicted me.

Lord, when David calls out to You, I hope that You hear me too.

April 28

1 Thessalonians 5:8 (NIV 1984)

⁸ But since we belong to the day, let us be self-controlled, putting on faith and love as a breastplate, and the hope of salvation as a helmet.

Lord, thank You for Your full suite of provision and protection.

April 29

Proverbs 3:3 (NIV 1984)

³ Let love and faithfulness never leave you;
bind them around your neck,
write them on the tablet of your heart.

Lord, thank You for love and faithfulness. Lord, I will write them on the tablet of my heart.

PRAYER JOURNAL FOR THE GROWING CHRISTIAN

April 30

Psalm 86:15 (NIV 1984)

[15] But you, O Lord, are a compassionate and gracious God, slow to anger, abounding in love and faithfulness.

_____
_____
_____
_____
_____
_____
_____
_____
_____
_____
_____
_____
_____
_____
_____
_____
_____

Lord, I do not know which I am more grateful for the most: Your compassion or Your love, Your grace or Your faithfulness.

Love

Such a powerful subject: LOVE! Love is a verb. It is what you do. Love is communicated through your actions, not just your words.

Love is defined by God and Jesus. "For God so loved the world that He gave His only begotten Son (John 3:16 NIV)." That is the definition of love. "While we were yet sinners, Christ died for our sins. (Romans 5:8)." That is the definition of love.

Giving us His Son and dying on the Cross are actions that articulate love. So as we seek to impose limits and boundaries on love of others, please be clear that the expectations are shallow as compared to what they have done to show Their love. Now that we have established the definition of love, we can all align ourselves accordingly.

In that alignment, we need to review 1 Corinthians 13 and 14. The verses are Paul's instructions about love. Replace 'love' with your name in the scriptures. As you consider your name as you replace love, is that statement true about you? If that sentence is not true, then how can we usher it toward truth. This is a great time to be honest with yourself. Once we are honest with ourselves, then we can be honest with others. Further, once we have revealed to ourselves our areas of need for love then we can better receive love and be more loving to others. The ultimate is being able to receive God's love at the best possible level.

The love God has for us is the most transparent, sacrificial love EVER. When I am most comfortable with His love, then I can obey, pray, serve, minister, and love. As an example of how authentic God's love is, I can tell you when I first did the name replacement in scripture, I cried for an hour. Those tears represented all the hurt, harm, danger and lack of forgiveness that I had experienced and had done to others in my lifetime. Those tears started an internal healing where I could muster an authentic love.

Consider a life with love. Full of love! Love allows you to relax. Love allows you to share your life with others in an authentic manner. The people around us and in our path are expecting our love for three reasons. Christians are expected to love by non-believers. Strangers expect love even though they are suspicious. People we do not know hope for our love but do not expect it. If we love others—ALL others—then God, and especially Jesus, will be pleased. Let us make Him proud. Let's love without being reminded or reprimanded.

May 1

Deuteronomy 6:5 (NIV 1984)

⁵ Love the LORD your God with all your heart and with all your soul and with all your strength.

Lord, I know that I love You with reservations and conditions. I am going to give You more of myself. Immediately.

May 2

John 3:16 (NIV 1984)

[16] "For God so loved the world that He gave His one and only Son, that whoever believes in Him shall not perish but have eternal life.

_____
_____
_____
_____
_____
_____
_____
_____
_____
_____
_____
_____
_____
_____
_____
_____
_____
_____
_____

Lord, that is love! The Only definition which matters and the Only one which will ever stand the test of time. Thank You so much!

May 3

1 Corinthians 13 (MSG)

The Way of Love

¹ If I speak with human eloquence and angelic ecstasy but don't love, I'm nothing but the creaking of a rusty gate.

² If I speak God's Word with power, revealing all his mysteries and making everything plain as day, and if I have faith that says to a mountain, "Jump," and it jumps, but I don't love, I'm nothing.

³⁻⁷ If I give everything I own to the poor and even go to the stake to be burned as a martyr, but I don't love, I've gotten nowhere. So, no matter what I say, what I believe, and what I do, I'm bankrupt without love.

Love never gives up.
Love cares more for others than for self.
Love doesn't want what it doesn't have.
Love doesn't strut,
Doesn't have a swelled head,
Doesn't force itself on others,
Isn't always "me first,"
Doesn't fly off the handle,
Doesn't keep score of the sins of others,
Doesn't revel when others grovel,
Takes pleasure in the flowering of truth,
Puts up with anything,
Trusts God always,
Always looks for the best,
Never looks back,
But keeps going to the end.

⁸⁻¹⁰ Love never dies. Inspired speech will be over some day; praying in tongues will end; understanding will reach its limit. We know only a portion of the truth, and what we say about God is always incomplete. But when the Complete arrives, our incompletes will be canceled.

[11] When I was an infant at my mother's breast, I gurgled and cooed like any infant. When I grew up, I left those infant ways for good.

[12] We don't yet see things clearly. We're squinting in a fog, peering through a mist. But it won't be long before the weather clears and the sun shines bright! We'll see it all then, see it all as clearly as God sees us, knowing him directly just as he knows us!

[13] But for right now, until that completeness, we have three things to do to lead us toward that consummation: Trust steadily in God, hope unswervingly, love extravagantly. And the best of the three is love.

_____
_____
_____
_____
_____
_____
_____
_____
_____
_____
_____
_____
_____
_____
_____
_____

Lord, thank You for Your extravagant love!

May 4

Zephaniah 3:17 (NIV 1984)

[17] The LORD your God is with you,
he is mighty to save.
He will take great delight in you,
he will quiet you with his love,
he will rejoice over you with singing."

_____
_____
_____
_____
_____
_____
_____
_____
_____
_____
_____
_____
_____
_____
_____
_____
_____
_____
_____
_____

May 5

Deuteronomy 7:13 (NIV 1984)

[13] He will love you and bless you and increase your numbers. He will bless the fruit of your womb, the crops of your land—your grain, new wine and oil—the calves of your herds and the lambs of your flocks in the land that he swore to your forefathers to give you.

May 6

Deuteronomy 11:13 (NIV1984)

¹³ So if you faithfully obey the commands I am giving you today—to love the LORD your God and to serve Him with all your heart and with all your soul—

Lord, I am working to give You my total self—my heart, my mind, my body, my spirit, and my soul.

May 7

Joshua 22:5 (NIV 1984)

⁵ But be very careful to keep the commandment and the law that Moses the servant of the LORD gave you: to love the LORD your God, to walk in all his ways, to obey his commands, to hold fast to him and to serve him with all your heart and all your soul."

Because of my love for You, God, I am diligently working to keep Your commands, with all of my heart, and soul. They belong to You.

May 8

Psalm 18:1 (NIV 1984)

¹ I love you, O LORD, my strength.

I love You, Lord. You are indeed my Strength.

May 9

Psalm 23:6 (NIV 1984)

⁶ Surely goodness and love will follow me all the days of my life, and I will dwell in the house of the LORD forever.

_____
_____
_____
_____
_____
_____
_____
_____
_____
_____
_____
_____
_____
_____
_____
_____
_____
_____

Lord, admittedly there are times when I wonder what where the goodness and love are and then You something outrageous.

May 10

Psalm 33:5 (NIV 1984)

⁵ The LORD loves righteousness and justice;
the earth is full of His unfailing love.

_____
_____
_____
_____
_____
_____
_____
_____
_____
_____
_____
_____
_____
_____
_____
_____
_____
_____
_____
_____

Lord, thank You for Your unfailing love.

May 11

Psalm 103:11 (NIV 1984)

¹¹ For as high as the heavens are above the earth,
so great is His love for those who fear Him;

Lord, I love that Your love is great for me.

May 12

Psalm 103:4 (NIV 1984)

⁴ who redeems your life from the pit
and crowns you with love and compassion,

_____

Lord, thank You for redeeming my life from the pit I walked into by myself. Thank You for Your crown of love and compassion.

…
May 13

Psalm 36:5 (NIV 1984)

⁵ Your love, O LORD, reaches to the heavens,
your faithfulness to the skies.

Lord, thank You for Your unlimited love and faithfulness.

May 14

Psalm 86:13 (NIV 1984)

¹³ For great is your love toward me;
you have delivered me from the depths of the grave.

_____

Lord, I could have been dead but Your love save me from the inevitable grave.

May 15

Isaiah 61:8 (NIV 1984)

⁸ "For I, the LORD, love justice;
I hate robbery and iniquity.
In my faithfulness I will reward them
and make an everlasting covenant with them.

_____
_____
_____
_____
_____
_____
_____
_____
_____
_____
_____
_____
_____
_____
_____
_____

Lord, I am trying to stay on the side of righteousness and justice.

May 16

Isaiah 63:9 (NIV 1984)

⁹ In all their distress he too was distressed,
and the angel of his presence saved them.
In his love and mercy he redeemed them;
he lifted them up and carried them
all the days of old.

Lord, thank You for Your powerful redemption.

PRAYER JOURNAL FOR THE GROWING CHRISTIAN

May 17

Matthew 5:44 (NIV 1984)

[44] But I tell you: Love your enemies and pray for those who persecute you,

---

Lord, I hear You and desperately want to please You. This is quite possibly the hardest request that You make.

ONE DAY MORE THAN WE DESERVE

May 18

Matthew 17:5 (NIV 1984)

⁵ While he was still speaking, a bright cloud enveloped them, and a voice from the cloud said, "This is my Son, whom I love; with him I am well pleased. Listen to him!"

Lord, it cost Him something for You to be able to say that. Lord, I just want to please You.

May 19

Matthew 19:19 (NIV 1984)

¹⁹ honor your father and mother,' and 'love your neighbor as yourself.'

Lord, I have a hard time with the love your neighbor part because sometimes I have trouble loving myself.

May 20

Luke 6:32 (NIV 1984)

[32] "If you love those who love you, what credit is that to you? Even 'sinners' love those who love them.

Lord, I am working to love those who do not love me. Please help me because You sent those to me to love.

May 21

John 13:34-35 (NIV 1984)

[34] "A new command I give you: Love one another. As I have loved you, so you must love one another. [35] By this all men will know that you are my disciples, if you love one another."

_____
_____
_____
_____
_____
_____
_____
_____
_____
_____
_____
_____
_____
_____
_____
_____
_____

Jesus, Your profound love is not transferable without much prayer. Help me to love like You continue to do.

May 22

John 14:15 (NIV 1984)

¹⁵ "If you love me, you will obey what I command.

I am having trouble in this area, Lord. Please help and guide.

Prayer Journal for the Growing Christian

May 23

John 15:13 (NIV 1984)

[13] Greater love has no one than this, that he lay down his life for his friends.

_____
_____
_____
_____
_____
_____
_____
_____
_____
_____
_____
_____
_____
_____
_____
_____
_____
_____
_____

Lord, I am sure that I could lay down my life for my friends.

One Day More Than We Deserve

May 24

Romans 5:5 (NIV 1984)

⁵ And hope does not disappoint us, because God has poured out His love into our hearts by the Holy Spirit, whom he has given us.

Lord, I do know that I am not the replenisher of my love tank. I know that You fill it so that I can love You, myself and others. Thank You.

May 25

Romans 5:8 (NIV 1984)

[8] But God demonstrates His own love for us in this: While we were still sinners, Christ died for us.

Lord, You have done so much to demonstrate Your love for me; this above all—yet I still have an issue loving You completely. Help me.

May 26

Romans 8:28 (NIV 1984)

[28] And we know that in all things God works for the good of those who love him, who have been called according to his purpose.

Lord, thank You for making sure that all things are working out for my good.

May 27

1 Corinthians 16:14 (NIV 1984)

[14] Do everything in love.

I will continue to all things because I love You, God, even it is conditional.

May 28

2 Corinthians 5:14 (NIV 1984)

¹⁴ For Christ's love compels us, because we are convinced that one died for all, and therefore all died.

_____

For the love You have for me, Jesus, I am compelled to make You pleased with me.

May 29

Ephesians 3:17-19 (NIV1984)

[17] so that Christ may dwell in your hearts through faith. And I pray that you, being rooted and established in love, [18] may have power, together with all the saints, to grasp how wide and long and high and deep is the love of Christ, [19] and to know this love that surpasses knowledge—that you may be filled to the measure of all the fullness of God.

Lord, the infinity of Your love makes me cry every time I read these verses and match them with my testimony.

One Day More Than We Deserve

May 30

Psalm 103:8 (NIV 1984)

⁸ The L%%ORD%% is compassionate and gracious,
slow to anger, abounding in love.

_____
_____
_____
_____
_____
_____
_____
_____
_____
_____
_____
_____
_____
_____
_____
_____
_____
_____
_____
_____

Lord, thank You for Your abounding love.

May 31

1 Peter 4:8 (NIV 1984)

⁸ Above all, love each other deeply, because love covers over a multitude of sins.

_____
_____
_____
_____
_____
_____
_____
_____
_____
_____
_____
_____
_____
_____
_____
_____
_____

Lord, allow me to love without reservation regardless of what I may not receive in return.

Prayer

Just a little talk with Jesus! Jesus taught the disciples how to pray. In this prayer, Jesus showed us how to adore God, honor God, ask for forgiveness and petition our needs. It is not a long prayer, however, it is precise and comprehensive. It is the foundations of all prayer.

Prayer is a decisive ordinance to God. Prayer is your communication with God. Prayer is your communication with God. Prayer is what we do to tell God how we feel and what we need and apologize for what we have done. Prayer is God's time to tell us what He needs from us, what He expects from us and His plans for us. Prayer is a point of enlightenment for us. Prayer is a measure of our transparency. Can you share ALL with God? He knows anyway. Your sharing is an act of reverence and obedience.

Why do I pray? There are several reasons why I pray. I am encouraging you to pray. So here are the reasons:

- Because God said to
- Because Jesus did
- Because prayer communicates love to God
- Because prayer is fuel for your soul
- Because prayer facilitates the growth in our relationship with God
- Because God wants to hear from me. He lifts my self-esteem when I share me with Him.
- Because He loves me and wants the best for me
- Because He deserves my time and energy and effort

- Because when I cry before Him, He cares and He offered me a place for my burdens: Him
- Because He can SOLVE those problems
- Because He gives me peace; His place which is at best incomprehensible

Prayer is the authentic dialogue you desire with others but can only have with God. I can tell God all that is on my mind and my heart. I can ask Him questions. I will get answers.

God loves me! Prayer is part of that love and affection God offers me.

Why would you not pray? It is the most authentic conversation you have with Someone who truly loves you. That same Someone who created you. That same Someone who provides for you. And protects you.

Prayer is essential. Keep praying.

June 1

Deuteronomy 4:7 (NIV 1984)

⁷ What other nation is so great as to have their gods near them the way the LORD our God is near us whenever we pray to him?

Thank You for being near me, God.

June 2

1 Samuel 12:23 (NIV 1984)

²³ As for me, far be it from me that I should sin against the LORD by failing to pray for you. And I will teach you the way that is good and right.

_____
_____
_____
_____
_____
_____
_____
_____
_____
_____
_____
_____
_____
_____
_____
_____
_____
_____
_____

Thank You for assigning people to pray for me.

June 3

2 Chronicles 7:14 (NIV 1984)

[14] if my people, who are called by my name, will humble themselves and pray and seek my face and turn from their wicked ways, then will I hear from heaven and will forgive their sin and will heal their land.

Lord, I will humble myself, and pray. Please heal me and my land.

June 4

Job 42:8 (NIV 1984)

⁸ So now take seven bulls and seven rams and go to my servant Job and sacrifice a burnt offering for yourselves. My servant Job will pray for you, and I will accept his prayer and not deal with you according to your folly. You have not spoken of me what is right, as my servant Job has."

Thank You for the people who pray for me, Father. I hope that I am trusted to pray for others.

June 5

Matthew 5:44 (NIV 1984)

[44] But I tell you: Love your enemies and pray for those who persecute you,

___

Lord, that is the hardest job ever! I am going to do it as often as I can remember; I promise to do better.

Prayer Journal for the Growing Christian

June 6

Matthew 6:5-8 (NIV 1984)

Prayer

[5] "And when you pray, do not be like the hypocrites, for they love to pray standing in the synagogues and on the street corners to be seen by men. I tell you the truth, they have received their reward in full. [6] But when you pray, go into your room, close the door and pray to your Father, who is unseen. Then your Father, who sees what is done in secret, will reward you. [7] And when you pray, do not keep on babbling like pagans, for they think they will be heard because of their many words. [8] Do not be like them, for your Father knows what you need before you ask him.

_____
_____
_____
_____
_____
_____
_____
_____
_____
_____
_____
_____
_____
_____

Jesus, thank You for teaching me to pray.

June 7

Matthew 26:36 (NIV 1984)

Gethsemane

[36] Then Jesus went with his disciples to a place called Gethsemane, and he said to them, "Sit here while I go over there and pray."

Lord, I pray to be in agreement with others who pray.

June 8

Luke 6:28 (NIV1984)

[28] bless those who curse you, pray for those who mistreat you.

_____
_____
_____
_____
_____
_____
_____
_____
_____
_____
_____
_____
_____
_____
_____
_____
_____
_____
_____
_____

Father God, I pray that they stop persecuting me.

June 9

Luke 18:1 (NIV 1984)

Then Jesus told his disciples a parable to show them that they should always pray and not give up.

_____
_____
_____
_____
_____
_____
_____
_____
_____
_____
_____
_____
_____
_____
_____
_____
_____
_____

Lord, I need that lesson now. I need to pray and not quit.

June 10

Luke 22:40 (NIV 1984)

⁴⁰ On reaching the place, He said to them, "Pray that you will not fall into temptation."

_____
_____
_____
_____
_____
_____
_____
_____
_____
_____
_____
_____
_____
_____
_____
_____
_____
_____
_____
_____

Jesus, please help me not to yield to temptation.

June 11

Romans 8:26 (NIV 1984)

²⁶ In the same way, the Spirit helps us in our weakness. We do not know what we ought to pray for, but the Spirit himself intercedes for us with groans that words cannot express.

Father, thank You for the Holy Spirit so that my prayer can be heard by You.

PRAYER JOURNAL FOR THE GROWING CHRISTIAN

June 12

Matthew 6:9—14 (NIV1984)

⁹ "This, then, is how you should pray:

"'Our Father in heaven,
hallowed be your name,
¹⁰ your kingdom come,
your will be done
on earth as it is in heaven.
¹¹ Give us today our daily bread.
¹² Forgive us our debts,
as we also have forgiven our debtors.
¹³ And lead us not into temptation,
but deliver us from the evil one.'

¹⁴ For if you forgive men when they sin against you, your heavenly Father will also forgive you. ¹⁵ But if you do not forgive men their sins, your Father will not forgive your sins.

_____
_____
_____
_____
_____
_____
_____
_____
_____
_____

Thank You, Jesus for this prayer of supplication to You.

June 13

1 Thessalonians 5:17 (NIV 1984)

[17] pray continually;

Thank You, Father, for being able to pray continually.

June 14

James 5:16 (NIV 1984)

[16] Therefore confess your sins to each other and pray for each other so that you may be healed. The prayer of a righteous man is powerful and effective.

_____
_____
_____
_____
_____
_____
_____
_____
_____
_____
_____
_____
_____
_____
_____
_____
_____

Thank You for showing me who I can confess my sins to, Father.

June 15

1 Samuel 1:27 (NIV 1984)

²⁷ I prayed for this child, and the LORD has granted me what I asked of him.

Lord, thank You for sharing when You grant Your will according to my prayers.

June 16

Jonah 2:1 (NIV)

[1] From inside the fish Jonah prayed to the LORD his God.

Lord, thank You for hearing my pray from anywhere.

June 17

Mark 14:35 (NIV)

³⁵ Going a little farther, He fell to the ground and prayed that if possible the hour might pass from him.

Jesus, thank You for showing me how to pray.

June 18

1 Chronicles 5:20 (NIV)

[20] They were helped in fighting them, and God delivered the Hagrites and all their allies into their hands, because they cried out to him during the battle. He answered their prayers, because they trusted in him.

_____
_____
_____
_____
_____
_____
_____
_____
_____
_____
_____
_____
_____
_____
_____
_____

Lord, thank You for teaching me that my prayers mean that I trust You.

ONE DAY MORE THAN WE DESERVE

June 19

Mark 11:24-25 (NIV)

²⁴ Therefore I tell you, whatever you ask for in prayer, believe that you have received it, and it will be yours. ²⁵ And when you stand praying, if you hold anything against anyone, forgive them, so that your Father in heaven may forgive you your sins."

___

Jesus, thank You for Your authority to use Your name in prayer. Thank You for Your gifts.

June 20

1 Peter 3:7 (NIV)

⁷ Husbands, in the same way be considerate as you live with your wives, and treat them with respect as the weaker partner and as heirs with you of the gracious gift of life, so that nothing will hinder your prayers.

_____
_____
_____
_____
_____
_____
_____
_____
_____
_____
_____
_____
_____
_____
_____
_____
_____

Jesus, thank You for helping me so that nothing hinders my prayers.

June 21

John 17:9, 15 (NIV)

⁹ I pray for them. I am not praying for the world, but for those you have given me, for they are yours.

¹⁵ My prayer is not that you take them out of the world but that you protect them from the evil one.

Jesus, thank You, for praying for my protection from the evil one.

PRAYER JOURNAL FOR THE GROWING CHRISTIAN

June 22

Acts 16:25 (NIV)

²⁵ About midnight Paul and Silas were praying and singing hymns to God, and the other prisoners were listening to them.

_____
_____
_____
_____
_____
_____
_____
_____
_____
_____
_____
_____
_____
_____
_____
_____
_____

Thank You, Jesus, for reminding me that others are listening to my reverence when I pray, praise and worship You.

June 23

Ephesians 6:18 (NIV)

¹⁸ And pray in the Spirit on all occasions with all kinds of prayers and requests. With this in mind, be alert and always keep on praying for all the Lord's people.

_____
_____
_____
_____
_____
_____
_____
_____
_____
_____
_____
_____
_____
_____
_____
_____
_____

Lord, thank You for the people who place in my path and the sensitivity and compassion You have gifted me with to pray for them.

June 24

Ephesians 3:14-21 (NIV)

A Prayer for the Ephesians

¹⁴ For this reason I kneel before the Father, ¹⁵ from whom every family in heaven and on earth derives its name. ¹⁶ I pray that out of his glorious riches he may strengthen you with power through his Spirit in your inner being, ¹⁷ so that Christ may dwell in your hearts through faith. And I pray that you, being rooted and established in love,

_____

_____

_____

_____

_____

_____

_____

_____

_____

_____

_____

_____

_____

_____

Lord, thank You for the example of Paul for me as a mighty prayer warrior.

June 25

Ephesians 3:18-21 (NIV)

[18] may have power, together with all the Lord's holy people, to grasp how wide and long and high and deep is the love of Christ, [19] and to know this love that surpasses knowledge—that you may be filled to the measure of all the fullness of God.

[20] Now to him who is able to do immeasurably more than all we ask or imagine, according to his power that is at work within us, [21] to him be glory in the church and in Christ Jesus throughout all generations, for ever and ever! Amen.

_____
_____
_____
_____
_____
_____
_____
_____
_____
_____
_____
_____
_____
_____

Thank You, Lord for Paul and the pray warrior he is. I pray that I pray for others as You have ordered.

June 26

Ezra 8:23 (NIV)

[23] So we fasted and petitioned our God about this, and He answered our prayer.

___

Lord, I pray to be attentive to Your voice and Your urgings that I may pray and fast at the proper time according to Your will.

One Day More Than We Deserve

June 27

Philippians 4:6 (NIV)

⁶ Do not be anxious about anything, but in every situation, by prayer and petition, with thanksgiving, present your requests to God.

___

Thank You for reminding me God to present everything to You, not choosing to omit issues because of how I think You will respond.

PRAYER JOURNAL FOR THE GROWING CHRISTIAN

June 28

Isaiah 56:7 (NIV)

⁷these I will bring to my holy mountain
and give them joy in my house of prayer.
Their burnt offerings and sacrifices
will be accepted on my altar;
for my house will be called
a house of prayer for all nations."

_____
_____
_____
_____
_____
_____
_____
_____
_____
_____
_____
_____
_____
_____
_____
_____

Thank You, God, for Your house of pray; may I dwell there always.

June 29

Proverbs 15:8 (NIV)

⁸ The LORD detests the sacrifice of the wicked,
but the prayer of the upright pleases him.

___

Lord, I want to be upright so that I can please You. I want You to be happy with me.

June 30

Matthew 6:16 (NIV)

Fasting

[16] "When you fast, do not look somber as the hypocrites do, for they disfigure their faces to show others they are fasting. Truly I tell you, they have received their reward in full.

_____
_____
_____
_____
_____
_____
_____
_____
_____
_____
_____
_____
_____
_____
_____

Lord, thank You for teaching me how to fast and pray. May my sacrifice bless Your will.

Heart

The heart is the source of your deepest emotions and the perfect hiding place for your fears and your wishes. The heart drives the ambitions we have. The heart is the expression of who we are.

Deuteronomy 4:29 reads: "But if from there you seek the LORD your God, you will find Him if you seek Him with all your heart and with all your soul."

With your heart, you love, grieve, and pursue your passions. For that reasons, the heart is critical. The heart is a critical element for what we do. The heart is the source of so much influence. Keep in mind, yearning starts in the heart. What we are called to do and designed to do will be fueled by the heart. This heart can be blamed and otherwise responsible for our achievements and accomplishments.

The heart is the fuel for so many situational instances. The heart forms the pattern of behavior and response based on experience. The problem we have is that we let the wrong "stuff" infect our hearts. Our hearts have been infected by offering access to the wrong persons and events. We refer to the fact that we have had our hearts broken which means that our hearts have been hurt and damaged—so much so that your heart had been paralyzed and altered.

The Source off all that we have is God. Our hearts needs to be RETURNED to God. We took the heart from God, allowed access to the wrong persons and events to distract us from Him and we relied on our personal frailness. These are all mistakes!

God is the author of our hearts. God is the restorer of our hearts. God is invested in the health of our hearts. We need to give it back it Him. I know it's broken and harmed, hard and bruised, and almost recognizable! God is a God of restoration! God can and will fix and restore your heart. He is entirely motivated to restore your heart because He needs it for His work and His glory.

God needs your heart whole and He is the only one who can heal it from the brokenness it has endured.

As you pray, ask God for healing and restoration. BELIEVE that He has healed. STOP retelling the story of how your heart broke and reminding yourself of the pain. Healing can not happen if you keep repeating the process.

Give your heart back to God. Put it back in His hands. Allow Him to guide it where it should go, love, trust, respect and learn.

God made your heart powerful for Him!

July 1

Joel 2:13 (NIV)

¹³ Rend your heart
and not your garments.
Return to the LORD your God,
for He is gracious and compassionate,
slow to anger and abounding in love,
and he relents from sending calamity.

Lord, thank You for being able to return to You. I left our relationship.

July 2

Leviticus 19:17 (NIV)

¹⁷ "'Do not hate a fellow Israelite in your heart. Rebuke your neighbor frankly so you will not share in their guilt.

Lord, please help us to remove hate and to be neighborly.

July 3

Deuteronomy 4:29 (NIV)

²⁹ But if from there you seek the LORD your God, you will find him if you seek him with all your heart and with all your soul.

___

Lord, I seek You but not completely. Help me Lord, to seek You with all that You created me to be.

PRAYER JOURNAL FOR THE GROWING CHRISTIAN

July 4

Exodus 25:2 (NIV)

² "Tell the Israelites to bring me an offering. You are to receive the offering for Me from everyone whose heart prompts them to give.

Lord, thank You for teaching me to give with my heart, otherwise the gift does not matter to You.

July 5

Deuteronomy 11:18 (NIV)

¹⁸ Fix these words of Mine in your hearts and minds; tie them as symbols on your hands and bind them on your foreheads.

Lord, I pray to fix Your words permanently to my heart, my hands, and my mind. I will share them with others.

July 6

Joshua 22:5 (NIV)

⁵ But be very careful to keep the commandment and the law that Moses the servant of the LORD gave you: to love the LORD your God, to walk in obedience to Him, to keep His commands, to hold fast to Him and to serve Him with all your heart and with all your soul."

Lord, I pray to be more obedient to You.

July 7

1 Samuel 13:14 (NIV)

¹⁴ But now your kingdom will not endure; the LORD has sought out a man after His own heart and appointed him ruler of His people, because you have not kept the LORD's command."

Lord, I pray that my heart is righteous enough to gift Your kingdom, Your people, and Your gifts.

Prayer Journal for the Growing Christian

July 8

1 Samuel 16:7 (NIV)

⁷ But the LORD said to Samuel, "Do not consider his appearance or his height, for I have rejected him. The LORD does not look at the things people look at. People look at the outward appearance, but the LORD looks at the heart."

_____
_____
_____
_____
_____
_____
_____
_____
_____
_____
_____
_____
_____
_____
_____
_____

Lord, when You look at my heart, I pray that it leads me to excellence for You and Your kingdom.

July 9

2 Kings 23:3 (NIV)

³ The king stood by the pillar and renewed the covenant in the presence of the LORD—to follow the LORD and keep His commands, statutes and decrees with all his heart and all his soul, thus confirming the words of the covenant written in this book. Then all the people pledged themselves to the covenant.

I pray Lord that I keep Your decrees, commands, and statues so I can enter the covenant You have for me.

PRAYER JOURNAL FOR THE GROWING CHRISTIAN

July 10

Psalm 51:10 (NIV)

[10] Create in me a pure heart, O God,
and renew a steadfast spirit within me.

Lord, I really need You to create in me a clean and pure heart and renew a steadfast spirit within me.

One Day More Than We Deserve

July 11

Psalm 19:14 (NIV)

[14] May these words of my mouth and this meditation of my heart be pleasing in your sight, LORD, my Rock and my Redeemer.

Lord, I pray that the words of my mouth and the meditations of my heart be pleasing to You.

PRAYER JOURNAL FOR THE GROWING CHRISTIAN

July 12

Psalm 119:11 (NIV)

¹¹ I have hidden Your word in my heart that I might not sin against You.

_____
_____
_____
_____
_____
_____
_____
_____
_____
_____
_____
_____
_____
_____
_____
_____
_____

Lord, I hope that You can find Your words hidden in my heart—I want to stop sinning against You.

July 13

Proverbs 27:19 (NIV)

¹⁹ As water reflects the face,
so one's life reflects the heart.

_____
_____
_____
_____
_____
_____
_____
_____
_____
_____
_____
_____
_____
_____
_____
_____
_____
_____
_____

I pray that I do better with my heart and consequently my life so that I represent You better.

July 14

Ecclesiastes 8:5 (NIV)

⁵ Whoever obeys his command will come to no harm,
and the wise heart will know the proper time and procedure.

_____
_____
_____
_____
_____
_____
_____
_____
_____
_____
_____
_____
_____
_____
_____
_____
_____
_____
_____
_____
_____
_____

I pray that You give me a wise heart, God.

July 15

Isaiah 40:11 (NIV)

[11] He tends his flock like a shepherd:
He gathers the lambs in his arms
and carries them close to his heart;
he gently leads those that have young.

_____
_____
_____
_____
_____
_____
_____
_____
_____
_____
_____
_____
_____
_____
_____
_____
_____
_____

Lord, thank You for holding me close to Your heart.

PRAYER JOURNAL FOR THE GROWING CHRISTIAN

July 16

Isaiah 57:15 (NIV)

[15] For this is what the high and exalted One says—
he who lives forever, whose name is holy:
"I live in a high and holy place,
but also with the one who is contrite and lowly in spirit,
to revive the spirit of the lowly and to revive the heart of the contrite.

Thank You for helping me with my contrite heart, Lord.

July 17

Jeremiah 17:9 (NIV)

⁹ The heart is deceitful above all things
and beyond cure.
Who can understand it?

_____
_____
_____
_____
_____
_____
_____
_____
_____
_____
_____
_____
_____
_____
_____
_____
_____

Lord, help me to avoid deceit with my heart—I pray for its pureness.

PRAYER JOURNAL FOR THE GROWING CHRISTIAN

July 18

Jeremiah 29:13 (NIV)

[13] You will seek Me and find Me when you seek Me with all your heart.

Lord, help me seek You authentically with all of my heart.

ONE DAY MORE THAN WE DESERVE

July 19

Matthew 5:8 (NIV)

[8] Blessed are the pure in heart, for they will see God.

___

Lord, help me avoid those things which cause my heart to not be pure.

July 20

Psalm 66:18 (NIV)

[18] If I had cherished sin in my heart, the Lord would not have listened;

Help me Lord, to only cherish what is righteous and pure so that You can hear my feeble, but authentic prayer.

July 21

Psalm 139:23 (NIV)

²³ Search me, God, and know my heart; test me and know my anxious thoughts.

Lord, there are days when I cannot read or pray that scripture authentically because my heart is a disappointment to You. Lord, help remove my anxiety.

PRAYER JOURNAL FOR THE GROWING CHRISTIAN

July 22

Proverbs 3:5 (NIV)

[5] Trust in the LORD with all your heart and lean not on your own understanding;

Thank You, God for the ability to lean on You because my understanding is faulty at times.

July 23

Proverbs 4:23 (NIV)

²³ Above all else, guard your heart, for everything you do flows from it.

Lord, help me to protect the heart which loves and is compassion, which works and creates.

July 24

Romans 10:10 (NIV)

¹⁰ For it is with your heart that you believe and are justified, and it is with your mouth that you profess your faith and are saved.

Lord, it is with my heart that I am justified about Your salvation which is very important to me. Keep my heart.

July 25

1 Peter 1:23 (NIV)

[23] For you have been born again, not of perishable seed, but of imperishable, through the living and enduring word of God.

Lord, thank You for Your enduring love.

July 26

Ephesians 6:6 (NIV)

⁶ Obey them not only to win their favor when their eye is on you, but as slaves of Christ, doing the will of God from your heart.

_____
_____
_____
_____
_____
_____
_____
_____
_____
_____
_____
_____
_____
_____
_____
_____
_____
_____

Lord, keep the path from my heart pure and clear; its where You do Your best work in my life.

July 27

Colossians 3:1 (NIV)

¹ Since, then, you have been raised with Christ, set your hearts on things above, where Christ is, seated at the right hand of God.

Lord, help me to not be anxious in my heart and to keep my heart set on what is above: You!

July 28

Hebrews 3:8 (NIV)

⁸ do not harden your hearts as you did in the rebellion, during the time of testing in the wilderness,

---

Lord, keep me from those things which harden my heart.

July 29

1 John 3:20 (NIV)

[20] If our hearts condemn us, we know that God is greater than our hearts, and He knows everything.

Lord, You won't even let my heart condemn me.

July 30

2 Corinthians 3:3 (NIV)

³ You show that you are a letter from Christ, the result of our ministry, written not with ink but with the Spirit of the living God, not on tablets of stone but on tablets of human hearts.

_____
_____
_____
_____
_____
_____
_____
_____
_____
_____
_____
_____
_____
_____
_____
_____

Lord, I have served with the spirit of the living God written on my human heart—please allow others to see it that they may be drawn to You.

ONE DAY MORE THAN WE DESERVE

July 31

Deuteronomy 10:12 (NIV)

Fear the LORD

¹² And now, Israel, what does the LORD your God ask of you but to fear the LORD your God, to walk in obedience to Him, to love Him, to serve the LORD your God with all your heart and with all your soul,

Lord, if I give You my whole heart and it is not split between You and wrong, I will please You, I pray.

Praise & Worship

Praise and worship are often used interchangeably. Praise and worship are both about God. Praise is defined as the act of expressing approval and admiration by dictionary.com. Worship is reverent honor and homage paid to God as defined by dictionary.com. The definition of praise used worship to define praise. They are different even though they are used together. So do we adequately praise and worship God? My answer is no. I could share my adoration of God more than I do. I was created to praise. I was also created to worship. God deserves our praise. God has earned our worship. Simply because He is God.

Both require our total surrender to God. Praise and worship require that we love God through our storms. Authentic praise and worship happens at the most uncomfortable times. Consider the reverence and adoration as the ultimate exercise of faith.

As a personal testimony, I praise and worship is more consistent when I am in a storm or under "stress." This process is what God uses to stretch me. Likewise, it is a reminder that I still love Him and He definitely loves me.

As my ministry expands, the one reminder that lingers in the back of my mind is that others are watching my praise and worship. My adoration and respect are on display. Others measure their praise and worship by my definition and through my actions. I know because that is what I was told. While that is a great information, it only means that as I worship and praise, I influence others to do the same. A person watching me does not change how I worship. My worship and praise is not a performance. And neither is yours.

Please do not compare your praise and worship to anyone else's. Our personal experiences shape and influences our praise and worship. When you are admiring someone's worship, keep in mind that there were specific instances that happened so that he could worship and praise God at a level you admire. Please do not use the worship and praise of another to shape your praise and worship.

    Praise and worship is about relationship.

ONE DAY MORE THAN WE DESERVE

August 1

1 Chronicles 16:29 (NIV)

²⁹ Ascribe to the LORD the glory due His name;
bring an offering and come before Him.
Worship the LORD in the splendor of His holiness.

_____
_____
_____
_____
_____
_____
_____
_____
_____
_____
_____
_____
_____
_____
_____
_____
_____
_____
_____

Lord, I pray that my worship brings You splendor!

August 2

Psalm 95:6 (NIV)

⁶ Come, let us bow down in worship,
let us kneel before the LORD our Maker;

_____

Lord, I kneel before You in total submission.

August 3

Matthew 2:2 (NIV)

² and asked, "Where is the one who has been born king of the Jews? We saw His star when it rose and have come to worship Him."

Jesus, I pray to help others to find You.

August 4

John 4:24 (NIV)

[24] God is spirit, and His worshipers must worship in the Spirit and in truth."

Lord, I humbly submit my worship and praise to You.

August 5

Romans 12:1 (NIV)

A Living Sacrifice

¹ Therefore, I urge you, brothers and sisters, in view of God's mercy, to offer your bodies as a living sacrifice, holy and pleasing to God—this is your true and proper worship.

Lord, if I give my body over to You as a living sacrifice, my worship would be unquestionable or deniable.

# August 6

Exodus 15:2 (NIV 1984)

² The LORD is my strength and my song;
He has become my salvation.
He is my God, and I will praise Him,
my father's God, and I will exalt Him.

Lord, I pray to relentlessly worship You.

August 7

Psalm 147:1 (NIV 1984)

¹ Praise the LORD, How good it is to sing praises to our God, how pleasant and fitting to praise Him!

Lord, I enjoy worshipping You!

August 8

2 Samuel 22:50 (NIV 1984)

[50] Therefore I will praise You, O Lord, among the nations;
I will sing praises to Your name.

Lord, I will sing Your praises everywhere.

August 9

1 Chronicles 29:10 (NIV 1984)

David's Prayer

¹⁰ David praised the LORD in the presence of the whole assembly, saying,

"Praise be to You, O LORD,
God of our father Israel,
from everlasting to everlasting.

Lord, I will praise You forever!

August 10

Nehemiah 8:6 (NIV 1984)

⁶ Ezra praised the LORD, the great God; and all the people lifted their hands and responded, "Amen! Amen!" Then they bowed down and worshiped the LORD with their faces to the ground.

_____
_____
_____
_____
_____
_____
_____
_____
_____
_____
_____
_____
_____
_____
_____
_____
_____

Lord, help me become comfortable with worshipping You on my face without being embarrassed.

… ONE DAY MORE THAN WE DESERVE

August 11

Daniel 2:19 (NIV 1984)

¹⁹ During the night the mystery was revealed to Daniel in a vision. Then Daniel praised the God of heaven

I owe You more praise, Lord.

August 12

1 Peter 4:11 (NIV 1984)

¹¹ If anyone speaks, he should do it as one speaking the very words of God. If anyone serves, he should do it with the strength God provides, so that in all things God may be praised through Jesus Christ. To Him be the glory and the power for ever and ever. Amen.

_____
_____
_____
_____
_____
_____
_____
_____
_____
_____
_____
_____
_____
_____
_____
_____
_____
_____
_____
_____

Lord, may my work bring You glory and honor, as a result of my worship and praise.

August 13

Deuteronomy 32:3 (NIV 1984)

³ I will proclaim the name of the LORD.
Oh, praise the greatness of our God!

I proclaim and praise Your holy name, God.

August 14

1 Chronicles 16:25 (NIV 1984)

²⁵ For great is the LORD and most worthy of praise;
He is to be feared above all gods.

_____
_____
_____
_____
_____
_____
_____
_____
_____
_____
_____
_____
_____
_____
_____
_____
_____
_____
_____
_____
_____
_____

Lord, great You are and worthy of my praise!

August 15

Psalm 8:2 (NIV 1984)

² From the lips of children and infants You have ordained praise because of Your enemies, to silence the foe and the avenger.

Lord, I pray that my praise silences all enemies.

PRAYER JOURNAL FOR THE GROWING CHRISTIAN

August 16

Psalm 33:1 (NIV 1984)

¹ Sing joyfully to the LORD, you righteous;
it is fitting for the upright to praise Him.

Whether righteous of not, I praise Thee O Lord!

August 17

Psalm 34:1 (NIV 1984)

[1] I will extol the LORD at all times; His praise will always be on my lips.

Lord, I am praying that only praise come from my lips.

August 18

Psalm 48:1 (NIV 1984)

[1] Great is the LORD, and most worthy of praise,
in the city of our God, His holy mountain.

Only You deserve my praise, Dear God.

ONE DAY MORE THAN WE DESERVE

August 19

Psalm 68:19 (NIV 1984)

[19] Praise be to the Lord, to God our Savior, who daily bears our burdens.

Thank You, Lord, for bearing my burdens.

PRAYER JOURNAL FOR THE GROWING CHRISTIAN

August 20

Psalm 100:4 (NIV 1984)

⁴ Enter His gates with thanksgiving and His courts with praise; give thanks to Him and praise His name.

I will enter Your courts at all times with my praise, God.

August 21

Psalm 106:1 (NIV 1984)

¹ Praise the LORD. Give thanks to the LORD, for He is good;
His love endures forever.

_____
_____
_____
_____
_____
_____
_____
_____
_____
_____
_____
_____
_____
_____
_____
_____
_____
_____
_____

Lord, thank You for Your love, which endures forever.

August 22

Psalm 119:175 (NIV 1984)

¹⁷⁵ Let me live that I may praise You, and may Your laws sustain me.

_____
_____
_____
_____
_____
_____
_____
_____
_____
_____
_____
_____
_____
_____
_____
_____
_____
_____
_____
_____

I live to praise You, God, and Your laws sustain me.

ONE DAY MORE THAN WE DESERVE

August 23

Psalm 139:14 (NIV 1984)

¹⁴ I praise you because I am fearfully and wonderfully made; your works are wonderful, I know that full well.

Some days I do not feel that I am fearfully or wonderfully made, but then God You remind me of why it is true. I will praise even when I do not feel like I deserve the life You so effortlessly provide.

PRAYER JOURNAL FOR THE GROWING CHRISTIAN

August 24

Psalm 145:1 (NIV 1984)

[1] I will exalt you, my God the King; I will praise Your name for ever and ever.

___

Lord, my life makes it easy to extol You.

August 25

Psalm 150:6 (NIV 1984)

⁶ Let everything that has breath praise the LORD. Praise the LORD.

My breath is enough reason to praise You, Lord.

August 26

Hebrews 13:15 (NIV 1984)

[15] Through Jesus, therefore, let us continually offer to God a sacrifice of praise—the fruit of lips that confess His name.

_____
_____
_____
_____
_____
_____
_____
_____
_____
_____
_____
_____
_____
_____
_____
_____
_____
_____
_____
_____

Lord, my verbal praise is truly deserved.

ONE DAY MORE THAN WE DESERVE

August 27

Matthew 5:16 (NIV 1984)

¹⁶ In the same way, let your light shine before men, that they may see your good deeds and praise your Father in heaven.

I hope that I let my light for You enough to please You, Father.

August 28

Ephesians 1:6 (NIV 1984)

⁶ to the praise of His glorious grace, which He has freely given us in the One He loves.

_____
_____
_____
_____
_____
_____
_____
_____
_____
_____
_____
_____
_____
_____
_____
_____
_____
_____
_____
_____

Lord, thank You for Your freely given, no strings attached grace.

August 29

Ephesians 1:12 (NIV 1984)

¹² in order that we, who were the first to hope in Christ, might be for the praise of His glory.

___

Lord, I offer You my praise. That is all that I have.

August 30

Deuteronomy 32:3 (NIV 1984)

³ I will proclaim the name of the LORD.
Oh, praise the greatness of our God!

Lord, I do not have full knowledge of Your greatness, yet I praise You.

August 31

Luke 4:8 (NIV 1984)

⁸ Jesus answered, "It is written: 'Worship the Lord your God and serve Him only.'"

I will only worship and serve You, God.

ONE DAY MORE THAN WE DESERVE

Forgiveness

Based on the temperament of the average person, forgiveness is not freely given. We have all held a grudge. It happens. The hurt is deeper than we realize and we need to forgive to start the healing process.

In the verses when Jesus teaches us to pray, Matthew 6:12 (NIV) reads "forgive us our sins as we forgive those who sin against us." Matthew 6:14-15 (KJV) reads "[14]For if ye forgive man their trespass, your heavenly Father will also forgive you. [15]But if ye forgive not men their trespasses, neither will your Father forgive your trespasses."

God is the Judge and Jury on this one. It is in plain English, in black and white—whatever cliché you use. OUCH! This means me too. I am not great at grudges but that does not mean I eagerly forgive. I am writing and considering what I do rather than eagerly forgive—I ignore the person and the circumstances. I distance myself quite well. Maybe your story resembles mine, however that means we are wrong. We are not forgiving. We are not being forgiven.

I have a lot of sins. All of which I need forgiveness for. I cannot afford to be unforgiven! If I want to be forgiven, I have to be a FORGIVER. This is a non-negotiable.

Jesus also teaches us that we have to forgive repeatedly. Peter asks Jesus in Matthew 18:21: "Lord, how many times shall I forgive my brother when he sins against me? Up to seven times?" Peter, like me, is looking for a way out. However, Jesus does not offer what Peter seeks. Matthew 18:22: "Jesus answered, "I tell you, not seven times, but seventy-seven times."

Forgiveness requires love. Not exactly love for a specific person but for us to be the definition of love. 1 Corinthians 13:5 reads: "[Love] is not rude, it is not self-seeking, it is not easily angered, [love] keeps no records of wrongs." We have to be love to forgive seventy-seven times and keep no record of wrong. So by conclusion, those "seventy-seven" times of forgiveness should be considered as unlimited. God forgets our sins (Isaiah 43:25) and as far as the east is from the west (Psalm 103:12).

Forgiveness is a matter of heart. Forgive and let God do the healing. The person who wronged you cannot fix the harm they have caused you.

September 1

2 Chronicles 7:14 (NIV 1984)

[14] if my people, who are called by my name, will humble themselves and pray and seek my face and turn from their wicked ways, then will I hear from heaven and will forgive their sin and will heal their land.

Lord, thank You for Your forgiveness.

September 2

Psalm 19:12 (NIV 1984)

¹² But who can discern their own errors? Forgive my hidden faults.

Lord, forgive my hidden faults. Lord, let me be receptive when You reveal the secrets.

September 3

Matthew 6:12 (NIV 1984)

¹² Forgive us our debts,
as we also have forgiven our debtors.

Lord, help me to forgive. I cannot afford You to withhold Your forgiveness.

PRAYER JOURNAL FOR THE GROWING CHRISTIAN

September 4

Matthew 6:14 (NIV 1984)

[14] For if you forgive men when they sin against you, your heavenly Father will also forgive you.

_____

Lord, I want to be able to forgive others freely.

ONE DAY MORE THAN WE DESERVE

September 5

Matthew 18:21 (NIV 1984)

[21] Then Peter came to Jesus and asked, "Lord, how many times shall I forgive my brother when he sins against me? Up to seven times?"

Lord, help me to forgive often—at least more than once.

September 6

Mark 11:25 (NIV 1984)

[25] And when you stand praying, if you hold anything against anyone, forgive him, so that your Father in heaven may forgive you your sins."

Lord, I cannot let my inability to forgive prevent my prayers being heard and answered.

One Day More Than We Deserve

September 7

Luke 11:4 (NIV 1984)

⁴ Forgive us our sins, for we also forgive everyone who sins against us. And lead us not into temptation.'"

Lord, help me away from temptation.

September 8

Luke 23:34 (NIV 1984)

³⁴ Jesus said, "Father, forgive them, for they do not know what they are doing." And they divided up His clothes by casting lots.

Jesus, I love You because You are THE example of what to do and how to respond to adversity.

September 9

Colossians 3:13 (NIV 1984)

¹³ Bear with each other and forgive whatever grievances you may have against one another. Forgive as the Lord forgave you.

Lord, I owe You so much in this area. I am too proud to forgive some of the people who should have been forgiven. Please help me with that matter—I need Your power.

PRAYER JOURNAL FOR THE GROWING CHRISTIAN

September 10

1 John 1:9 (NIV1984)

⁹ If we confess our sins, He is faithful and just and will forgive us our sins and purify us from all unrighteousness.

_____

Lord, thank You for purifying me from my unrighteousness.

September 11

Psalm 130:4 (NIV 1984)

⁴ But with you there is forgiveness; therefore you are feared.

_____

Lord, I know forgiving others would give me the power for which I prayed. Help me to forgive.

PRAYER JOURNAL FOR THE GROWING CHRISTIAN

September 12

Acts 10:43 (NIV 1984)

[43] All the prophets testify about Him that everyone who believes in Him receives forgiveness of sins through His name."

Thank You for Your name, Lord, and all that is a benefit of Your Holy name.

September 13

Ephesians 1:7 (NIV 1984)

⁷ In Him we have redemption through His blood, the forgiveness of sins, in accordance with the riches of God's grace

---

Lord, thank You for Your redemption, and forgiveness because of Your love.

PRAYER JOURNAL FOR THE GROWING CHRISTIAN

September 14

Colossians 1:13-14 (NIV 1984)

[13] For He has rescued us from the dominion of darkness and brought us into the kingdom of the Son He loves, [14] in whom we have redemption, the forgiveness of sins.

Lord, thank You from rescuing from the dominion of darkness and bringing me into the kingdom of Jesus.

September 15

Hebrews 9:22 (NIV 1984)

²² In fact, the law requires that nearly everything be cleansed with blood, and without the shedding of blood there is no forgiveness.

Lord, the blood You shed was enough.

September 16

Nehemiah 9:17 (NIV 1984)

[17] They refused to listen and failed to remember the miracles you performed among them. They became stiff-necked and in their rebellion appointed a leader in order to return to their slavery. But you are a forgiving God, gracious and compassionate, slow to anger and abounding in love.

Thank You, for Your abounding love and Your forgiveness.

September 17

Ephesians 4:32 (NIV 1984)

³² Be kind and compassionate to one another, forgiving each other, just as in Christ God forgave you.

Lord, help me to fulfill this command. It is so hard to be compassionate to others when they are not working within in my unauthorized boundaries.

September 18

Micah 7:18 (NIV 1984)

¹⁸ Who is a God like you,
who pardons sin and forgives the transgression
of the remnant of his inheritance?
You do not stay angry forever
but delight to show mercy.

Lord, I am definitely not like You: I do not forgive quickly nor am I quick to show mercy.

September 19

Genesis 50:17 (NIV 1984)

¹⁷ 'This is what you are to say to Joseph: I ask you to forgive your brothers the sins and the wrongs they committed in treating you so badly.' Now please forgive the sins of the servants of the God of your father." When their message came to him, Joseph wept.

Lord, Jacob is a great example of forgiveness and how to parent and to forgive.

September 20

Exodus 34:9 (NIV 1984)

⁹ "O Lord, if I have found favor in your eyes," he said, "then let the Lord go with us. Although this is a stiff-necked people, forgive our wickedness and our sin, and take us as your inheritance."

Thank You, Lord, for forgiving me of my wickedness and stiff-necked behavior.

September 21

Numbers 14:19-20 (NIV 1984)

[19] In accordance with Your great love, forgive the sin of these people, just as You have pardoned them from the time they left Egypt until now."

[20] The LORD replied, "I have forgiven them, as you asked.

Lord, forgive me. I need the same forgiveness the Israelites experienced.

September 22

1 Kings 8:36-39 (NIV 1984)

^{36} then hear from heaven and forgive the sin of your servants, your people Israel. Teach them the right way to live, and send rain on the land you gave your people for an inheritance.

^{37} "When famine or plague comes to the land, or blight or mildew, locusts or grasshoppers, or when an enemy besieges them in any of their cities, whatever disaster or disease may come, ^{38} and when a prayer or plea is made by any of your people Israel—each one aware of the afflictions of his own heart, and spreading out his hands toward this temple— ^{39} then hear from heaven, your dwelling place. Forgive and act; deal with each man according to all he does, since you know his heart (for you alone know the hearts of all men),

_____
_____
_____
_____
_____
_____
_____
_____
_____
_____
_____
_____

Lord, You are aware of the afflictions of my heart. Thank You for helping me to overcome those afflictions.

September 23

1 Kings 8:50 (NIV 1984)

⁵⁰ And forgive Your people, who have sinned against You; forgive all the offenses they have committed against You, and cause their conquerors to show them mercy;

Lord, I love You and thank You for Your forgiveness of my most egregious sins.

# September 24

2 Chronicles 6:39 (NIV 1984)

³⁹ then from heaven, Your dwelling place, hear their prayer and their pleas, and uphold their cause. And forgive Your people, who have sinned against You.

Lord, I am in desperate need of Your forgiveness.

ONE DAY MORE THAN WE DESERVE

September 25

Job 7:21 (NIV 1984)

²¹ Why do you not pardon my offenses and forgive my sins?
For I will soon lie down in the dust;
you will search for me, but I will be no more."

Lord, I feel like Job at times as well. I am working to be more in Your favor.

PRAYER JOURNAL FOR THE GROWING CHRISTIAN

September 26

Psalm 25:11 (NIV 1984)

¹¹ For the sake of Your name, O LORD, forgive my iniquity, though it is great.

_____
_____
_____
_____
_____
_____
_____
_____
_____
_____
_____
_____
_____
_____
_____
_____
_____
_____
_____

Forgive my great iniquities dear Father.

September 27

Psalm 32:1 (NIV 1984)

¹ Blessed is he whose transgressions are forgiven, whose sins are covered.

Lord, I am blessed that You forgive me.

September 28

Psalm 103 (NIV 1984)

[1] Praise the LORD, O my soul;
all my inmost being, praise His holy name.
[2] Praise the LORD, O my soul,
and forget not all His benefits—
[3] who forgives all your sins
and heals all your diseases,
[4] who redeems your life from the pit
and crowns you with love and compassion,
[5] who satisfies your desires with good things
so that your youth is renewed like the eagle's.

_____
_____
_____
_____
_____
_____
_____
_____
_____
_____
_____
_____
_____
_____

Lord, I praise Your Holy name.

September 29

Jeremiah 31:34 (NIV 1984)

³⁴ No longer will a man teach his neighbor,
or a man his brother, saying, 'Know the LORD,'
because they will all know me,
from the least of them to the greatest,"
declares the LORD.
"For I will forgive their wickedness
and will remember their sins no more."

Thank You Lord, for remembering my sins no more.

September 30

Jeremiah 33:8 (NIV 1984)

⁸ I will cleanse them from all the sin they have committed against Me and will forgive all their sins of rebellion against Me.

Lord, thank You for forgiving me for my rebellion.

Teaching

Jesus is a teacher. There is no doubt about it. Teaching is critical to the growth of every Christian. How do I know which teaching is good? How do I know that I am growing? These are two great questions for us to consider.

Sound teaching—sound doctrine—is based on the Bible. If you cannot find the foundation for the information you are being taught in the Bible, then you should consider that questionable. It may make sense, however good, gifted teachers use the Bible to teach and they share the scripture references as they do so. Likewise, when you need clarification or support, that same gifted teacher can and will offer Biblical references for your questions and concerns.

With prayer, meditation and study, growth should happen. This maybe incrementally realized and while studying, inevitable. Keep focuses on the you that God wants you to be. The growth will not be as obvious to you, yet subtle and constant until a full recovery has taken place. When you fully realize the growth, then you will share the testimony about your growth through the study of God's word while we are learning and praying and becoming closer to God, we will influence others to grow as well. Others will notice your growth and will then desire to do so as well. They may ask what you are doing, what specifically you are studying, so share what you are reading and the class(es) you are taking.

I am gifted as a teacher. I love Jesus as my Teacher for how to teach. Jesus spends time teaching the disciples with parables, prayer and demonstration. Jesus reinforces the teaching through His actions. Jesus does everything He expects of us. Jesus shares the essence of who God is and who God expects us to be. In His sharing and teaching, He is inclusive of all that He knows we will need in this life via actual application or by inference of the teaching. Jesus does not leave any details out of His teaching.

Further He teaches us how to live and co-exist with others in a manner that will please God. Jesus' teachings are concise and comprehensive. He lived 33 years an taught everyday—whether speaking or silent. He is our example. His teaching help us get closer to Him each day.

October 1

Exodus 33:13 (NIV 1984)

[13] If you are pleased with me, teach me Your ways so I may know You and continue to find favor with You. Remember that this nation is Your people."

_____
_____
_____
_____
_____
_____
_____
_____
_____
_____
_____
_____
_____
_____
_____
_____
_____
_____
_____
_____

Thank You, Lord, for teaching me Your ways.

October 2

Deuteronomy 4:9 (NIV 1984)

⁹ Only be careful, and watch yourselves closely so that you do not forget the things your eyes have seen or let them slip from your heart as long as you live. Teach them to your children and to their children after them.

Lord, I will teach my children, and my grandchildren, and my great-grandchildren.

October 3

Deuteronomy 8:3 (NIV 1984)

³ He humbled you, causing you to hunger and then feeding you with manna, which neither you nor your fathers had known, to teach you that man does not live on bread alone but on every word that comes from the mouth of the LORD.

___

Lord, thank You for providing me with Your word to live on. Thank You for teaching me to live only on Your word.

October 4

Deuteronomy 11:19 (NIV 1984)

[19] Teach them to your children, talking about them when you sit at home and when you walk along the road, when you lie down and when you get up.

Lord, I will teach my children Your word.

October 5

1 Samuel 12:23 (NIV 1984)

²³ As for me, far be it from me that I should sin against the LORD by failing to pray for you. And I will teach you the way that is good and right.

Thank You Lord, for teaching me the ways which are right and good.

October 6

Psalm 32:8 (NIV 1984)

⁸ I will instruct you and teach you in the way you should go;
I will counsel you and watch over you.

Lord, thank You for the teachings will cause me to change my motives.

October 7

Psalm 51:13 (NIV 1984)

¹³ Then I will teach transgressors your ways,
and sinners will turn back to you.

Lord, if You tell my transgressors my ways, then ways will change.

PRAYER JOURNAL FOR THE GROWING CHRISTIAN

October 8

Psalm 90:12 (NIV 1984)

¹² Teach us to number our days aright,
that we may gain a heart of wisdom.

_____
_____
_____
_____
_____
_____
_____
_____
_____
_____
_____
_____
_____
_____
_____
_____
_____
_____

Lord, teach me to number my days and not take any of them for granted. Thank You, for my heart of wisdom.

October 9

Psalm 143:10 (NIV 1984)

¹⁰ Teach me to do Your will,
for You are my God;
may Your good Spirit
lead me on level ground.

Lord, teach me to do Your will so that Your spirit can lead me to level ground.

PRAYER JOURNAL FOR THE GROWING CHRISTIAN

October 10

Luke 11:1 (NIV1984)

Jesus' Teaching on Prayer

[1] One day Jesus was praying in a certain place. When He finished, one of His disciples said to Him, "Lord, teach us to pray, just as John taught his disciples."

Thank You for teaching me to pray, Jesus.

October 11

John 14:26 (NIV 1984)

²⁶ But the Counselor, the Holy Spirit, whom the Father will send in My name, will teach you all things and will remind you of everything I have said to you.

Jesus, thank You for the Counselor and His teachings for me.

Prayer Journal for the Growing Christian

October 12

Titus 2:1 (NIV 1984)

[1] You must teach what is in accord with sound doctrine.

Remind me as I teach, Lord, to teach only sound doctrine.

October 13

James 3:1(NIV 1984)

¹ Not many of you should presume to be teachers, my brothers, because you know that we who teach will be judged more strictly.

Lord, I do not want to be responsible for their knowledge and understanding unless You have chosen me.

# October 14

1 John 2:27 (NIV 1984)

²⁷ As for you, the anointing you received from Him remains in you, and you do not need anyone to teach you. But as His anointing teaches you about all things and as that anointing is real, not counterfeit—just as it has taught you, remain in Him.

_____
_____
_____
_____
_____
_____
_____
_____
_____
_____
_____
_____
_____
_____
_____
_____
_____
_____
_____

Thank You for teaching me to remain in You, Christ.

October 15

Matthew 10:24 (NIV 1984)

[24] "A student is not above his teacher, nor a servant above his master.

Lord, help me keep my perspective, especially when You teach me new things.

… to be done more often, physically and metaphorically.

October 16

John 13:14 (NIV1984)

¹⁴ Now that I, your Lord and Teacher, have washed your feet, you also should wash one another's feet.

Lord, this is such a blessing, which needs to be done more often, physically and metaphorically.

October 17

1 Corinthians 12:28 (NIV 1984)

²⁸ And in the church God has appointed first of all apostles, second prophets, third teachers, then workers of miracles, also those having gifts of healing, those able to help others, those with gifts of administration, and those speaking in different kinds of tongues.

Thank You for the immeasurable gifts which You have gifted me, God.

October 18

Ephesians 4:11 (NIV 1984)

¹¹ It was He who gave some to be apostles, some to be prophets, some to be evangelists, and some to be pastors and teachers,

_____

Sometimes, God, I wonder what criteria You used to give me the gifts I have.

ONE DAY MORE THAN WE DESERVE

October 19

Hebrews 5:12 (NIV 1984)

¹² In fact, though by this time you ought to be teachers, you need someone to teach you the elementary truths of God's word all over again. You need milk, not solid food!

Thank You, God, for being patient as I continue to miss the opportunities to show You that I have matured by actually maturing.

October 20

1 Timothy 6:3 (NIV 1984)

³ If anyone teaches false doctrines and does not agree to the sound instruction of our Lord Jesus Christ and to godly teaching, ⁴ they are conceited and understand nothing. They have an unhealthy interest in controversies and quarrels about words that result in envy, strife, malicious talk, evil suspicions ⁵ and constant friction between people of corrupt mind, who have been robbed of the truth and who think that godliness is a means to financial gain.

_____
_____
_____
_____
_____
_____
_____
_____
_____
_____
_____
_____
_____
_____
_____
_____

Lord, help me to never to teach false doctrine or offend You with misunderstanding Your word.

October 21

Proverbs 1:8 (NIV 1984)

⁸ Listen, my son, to your father's instruction
and do not forsake your mother's teaching.

Lord, remind me even as an adult to seek and listen to wise teachings.

PRAYER JOURNAL FOR THE GROWING CHRISTIAN

October 22

Matthew 28:20 (NIV 1984)

[20] and teaching them to obey everything I have commanded you. And surely I am with you always, to the very end of the age."

Jesus, help me to teach them under whatever circumstances You provide. Thank You for trusting me.

ONE DAY MORE THAN WE DESERVE

October 23

John 7:17 (NIV 1984)

[17] If anyone chooses to do God's will, he will find out whether my teaching comes from God or whether I speak on my own.

You have made it plain that You are the real true Jesus, God's Son and Rock and My Redeemer.

Prayer Journal for the Growing Christian

October 24

John 14:23 (NIV 1984)

²³ Jesus replied, "If anyone loves Me, he will obey My teaching. My Father will love him, and We will come to him and make our home with him.

Thank You, God, for making a home with me.

October 25

1 Timothy 4:13 (NIV 1984)

[13] Until I come, devote yourself to the public reading of Scripture, to preaching and to teaching.

___

Lord, when You gave Paul a job, You gave us all a job. Thank You so much!

PRAYER JOURNAL FOR THE GROWING CHRISTIAN

October 26

2 Timothy 3:16 (NIV 1984)

[16] All Scripture is God-breathed and is useful for teaching, rebuking, correcting and training in righteousness,

Lord, thank You for such a mighty tool as Your Word.

October 27

Titus 2:7 (NIV 1984)

⁷ In everything set them an example by doing what is good. In your teaching show integrity, seriousness

Lord, thank You for helping me to teach with integrity.

October 28

John 3:1-2 (NIV 1984)

Jesus Teaches Nicodemus

3 Now there was a man of the Pharisees named Nicodemus, a member of the Jewish ruling council. ² He came to Jesus at night and said, "Rabbi, we know You are a teacher who has come from God. For no one could perform the miraculous signs You are doing if God were not with Him."

_____
_____
_____
_____
_____
_____
_____
_____
_____
_____
_____
_____
_____
_____
_____
_____

Teachers are assigned by God, thank You for the teachers who you have assigned to me.

October 29

John 3:10-11 (NIV 1984)

[10] "You are Israel's teacher," said Jesus, "and do you not understand these things? [11] I tell you the truth, we speak of what we know, and we testify to what we have seen, but still you people do not accept our testimony.

Lord, help others accept my testimony. It takes me so much to share, so I need it to be worth it.

October 30

Luke 2:46-47 (NIV 1984)

⁴⁶ After three days they found Him in the temple courts, sitting among the teachers, listening to them and asking them questions. ⁴⁷ Everyone who heard Him was amazed at His understanding and His answers.

Lord, let me be found working productively according to Your will.

October 31

1 Corinthians 2:13 (NIV 1984)

¹³ This is what we speak, not in words taught us by human wisdom but in words taught by the Spirit, expressing spiritual truths in spiritual words.

Lord, let me be sensitive to the movement and voice of the Holy Spirit.

PRAYER JOURNAL FOR THE GROWING CHRISTIAN

Discipleship

Jesus called us to make others' disciples. He made twelve. Those eleven were responsible for the rest of us. We are responsible for each other. Discipleship is training believers to train other believers. Disciples are responsible for teaching, sharing Jesus, and baptizing others in the name of Jesus.

The other part of discipleship is our responsibilities as a disciple. God expects us to be loving, faithful, prayer warriors, who teach about Him and are obedient to Him. Yes, we have a lot of work—DAILY.

Matthew 28:19-20 [19] Therefore go and make disciples of all nations, baptizing them in the name of the Father and of the Son and of the Holy Spirit, [20] and teaching them to obey everything I have commanded you. And surely I am with you always, to the very end of the age."

Luke 9:23 [23] Then he said to them all: "Whoever wants to be my disciple must deny themselves and take up their cross daily and follow me.

John 13:34-35 [34] "A new command I give you: Love one another. As I have loved you, so you must love one another. [35] By this everyone will know that you are my disciples, if you love one another."

Matthew 14:31 [31] Immediately Jesus reached out his hand and caught him. "You of little faith," he said, "why did you doubt?"

Matthew 26:36-37 [36] Then Jesus went with his disciples to a place called Gethsemane, and he said to them, "Sit here while I go over there and pray." [37] He took Peter and the two sons of Zebedee along with him, and he began to be sorrowful and troubled.

John 14:15 (John 14:21, 23, 24) [15] "If you love me, keep my commands. Jesus calls for disciples to serve others with compassion and care.

John 13:13-17 [13] "You call me 'Teacher' and 'Lord,' and rightly so, for that is what I am. [14] Now that I, your Lord and Teacher, have washed your feet, you also should wash one another's feet. [15] I have set you an example that you should do as I have done for you. [16] Very truly I tell you, no servant is greater than his master, nor is a messenger greater than the one who sent him. [17] Now that you know these things, you will be blessed if you do them.

John 11:33-35 [33] When Jesus saw her weeping, and the Jews who had come along with her also weeping, he was deeply moved in spirit and troubled. [34] "Where have you laid him?" he asked. "Come and see, Lord," they replied. [35] Jesus wept.

John 14:1-2

Jesus loves us and He commands us to love others. Jesus gives us a chance to do what He desires and to serve others.

November 1

John 2:7 (NIV 1984)

⁷ Jesus said to the servants, "Fill the jars with water"; so they filled them to the brim. ⁸ Then He told them, "Now draw some out and take it to the master of the banquet."

Jesus, You are going to ask me for many things which I do not understand. Help me to stay focused on You.

PRAYER JOURNAL FOR THE GROWING CHRISTIAN

November 2

John 2:18-19 (NIV 1984)

[18] Then the Jews demanded of Him, "What miraculous sign can you show us to prove Your authority to do all this?" [19] Jesus answered them, "Destroy this temple, and I will raise it again in three days."

Jesus, I love Your authority!

November 3

John 4:26, 29 (NIV)

²⁶ Then Jesus declared, "I, the One speaking to you—I am He."
²⁹"Come, see a man who told me everything I ever did. Could this be the Messiah?"

Jesus, I pray that people stop having the need to questions Your identity.

PRAYER JOURNAL FOR THE GROWING CHRISTIAN

November 4

John 4:48-50 (NIV)

⁴⁸ "Unless you people see signs and wonders," Jesus told him, "You will never believe." ⁴⁹ The royal official said, "Sir, come down before my child dies." ⁵⁰ "Go," Jesus replied, "Your son will live." The man took Jesus at His word and departed.

Jesus, I still need to see things which I should just believe because it is of You. Thank You!

November 5

John 5:6, 8 (NIV)

⁶ When Jesus saw him lying there and learned that he had been in this condition for a long time, He asked him, "Do you want to get well?" ⁸Then Jesus said to him, "Get up! Pick up your mat and walk."

Lord, I want to walk and be made whole.

PRAYER JOURNAL FOR THE GROWING CHRISTIAN

November 6

John 6:11 (NIV)

[11] Jesus then took the loaves, gave thanks, and distributed to those who were seated as much as they wanted. He did the same with the fish.

Jesus, Thank You for feeding me with what appear to be nothing.

One Day More Than We Deserve

November 7

John 6:20 (NIV)

[20] But He said to them, "It is I; don't be afraid."

Jesus, how often have I seen You and missed the moment to understand that You were present? I am working to never let that happen again.

PRAYER JOURNAL FOR THE GROWING CHRISTIAN

November 8

John 13:8 (NIV)

⁸ "No," said Peter, "You shall never wash my feet."
Jesus answered, "Unless I wash you, you have no part with Me."

Jesus, thank You for helping me to understand how to serve others.

ONE DAY MORE THAN WE DESERVE

November 9

John 13:21 (NIV)

²¹ After He had said this, Jesus was troubled in spirit and testified, "Very truly I tell you, one of you is going to betray Me."

_____
_____
_____
_____
_____
_____
_____
_____
_____
_____
_____
_____
_____
_____
_____
_____
_____
_____

Jesus, please do not allow me to betray You.

PRAYER JOURNAL FOR THE GROWING CHRISTIAN

November 10

John 13:38 (NIV)

[38] Then Jesus answered, "Will you really lay down your life for Me? Very truly I tell you, before the rooster crows, you will disown Me three times!

Christ, when this has been me, please forgive me!

ONE DAY MORE THAN WE DESERVE

November 11

Matthew 14:29-30 (NIV)

²⁹ "Come," He said. Then Peter got down out of the boat, walked on the water and came toward Jesus. ³⁰ But when he saw the wind, he was afraid and, beginning to sink, cried out, "Lord, save me!"

Jesus, thank You for inviting my out to walk on water.

PRAYER JOURNAL FOR THE GROWING CHRISTIAN

November 12

Matthew 13:19 (NIV)

[19] When anyone hears the message about the kingdom and does not understand it, the evil one comes and snatches away what was sown in their heart. This is the seed sown along the path.

_____
_____
_____
_____
_____
_____
_____
_____
_____
_____
_____
_____
_____
_____
_____
_____
_____
_____
_____

Jesus, please do not let the enemy come and snatch any of my learnings.

ONE DAY MORE THAN WE DESERVE

November 13

Matthew 16:25-26 (NIV)

²⁵ For whoever wants to save their life will lose it, but whoever loses their life for Me will find it. ²⁶ What good will it be for someone to gain the whole world, yet forfeit their soul? Or what can anyone give in exchange for their soul?

Jesus, thank You for helping me to understand what it takes to follow You.

PRAYER JOURNAL FOR THE GROWING CHRISTIAN

November 14

Matthew 18:12 (NIV)

¹² "What do you think? If a man owns a hundred sheep, and one of them wanders away, will he not leave the ninety-nine on the hills and go to look for the one that wandered off?

_____
_____
_____
_____
_____
_____
_____
_____
_____
_____
_____
_____
_____
_____
_____
_____
_____
_____

Jesus, thank You for teaching me to care for others and those for whom I am responsible.

November 15

Matthew 18:33 (NIV)

33 Shouldn't you have had mercy on your fellow servant just as I had on you?'

Jesus, thank You for reminding me how to treat others.

PRAYER JOURNAL FOR THE GROWING CHRISTIAN

November 16

Matthew 20:13-15 (NIV)

¹³ "But he answered one of them, 'I am not being unfair to you, friend. Didn't you agree to work for a denarius? ¹⁴ Take your pay and go. I want to give the one who was hired last the same as I gave you. ¹⁵Don't I have the right to do what I want with my own money? Or are you envious because I am generous?'

Lord, thank You for teaching me how to fair and equal are different.

November 17

Matthew 22:37 (NIV)

³⁷ Jesus replied: "'Love the Lord your God with all your heart and with all your soul and with all your mind.'

Jesus, thank You for reinforcing the love of God with all of me.

November 18

Luke 18:42 (NIV)

⁴² Jesus said to him, "Receive your sight; your faith has healed you."

Jesus, thank You for healing me when I am faithful.

November 19

Luke 14:33 (NIV)

[33] In the same way, those of you who do not give up everything you have cannot be my disciples.

Jesus, I am not sure that I made the discipleship criteria. Help me meet Your criteria.

PRAYER JOURNAL FOR THE GROWING CHRISTIAN

November 20

Luke 15:9 (NIV)

⁹ And when she finds it, she calls her friends and neighbors together and says, 'Rejoice with me; I have found my lost coin.'

Jesus, thank You for reminding me to rejoice with those who rejoice.

November 21

Luke 17:15 (NIV)

¹⁵ One of them, when he saw he was healed, came back, praising God in a loud voice.

Jesus, I owe You my praise at all times.

PRAYER JOURNAL FOR THE GROWING CHRISTIAN

November 22

Mark 13:35 (NIV)

³⁵ "Therefore keep watch because you do not know when the owner of the house will come back—whether in the evening, or at midnight, or when the rooster crows, or at dawn.

_____
_____
_____
_____
_____
_____
_____
_____
_____
_____
_____
_____
_____
_____
_____
_____
_____

Jesus, thank You for reminding me that I do know when You will return.

ONE DAY MORE THAN WE DESERVE

November 23

Matthew 28:16-20 (NIV)

The Great Commission

¹⁶ Then the eleven disciples went to Galilee, to the mountain where Jesus had told them to go. ¹⁷ When they saw him, they worshiped him; but some doubted. ¹⁸ Then Jesus came to them and said, "All authority in heaven and on earth has been given to me. ¹⁹ Therefore go and make disciples of all nations, baptizing them in the name of the Father and of the Son and of the Holy Spirit, ²⁰ and teaching them to obey everything I have commanded you. And surely I am with you always, to the very end of the age."

Jesus, thank You for such an overwhelming assignment.

November 24

Matthew 25:21 (NIV)

[21] "His master replied, 'Well done, good and faithful servant! You have been faithful with a few things; I will put you in charge of many things. Come and share your master's happiness!'

Jesus, I am anticipating the time when You are able to say this to me.

ONE DAY MORE THAN WE DESERVE

November 25

John 14:12-17, 18-20 (NIV)

¹² My command is this: Love each other as I have loved you. ¹³ Greater love has no one than this: to lay down one's life for one's friends. ¹⁴ You are my friends if you do what I command. ¹⁵ I no longer call you servants, because a servant does not know his master's business. Instead, I have called you friends, for everything that I learned from my Father I have made known to you. ¹⁶ You did not choose me, but I chose you and appointed you so that you might go and bear fruit—fruit that will last—and so that whatever you ask in my name the Father will give you. ¹⁷ This is my command: Love each other.

The World Hates the Disciples

¹⁸ "If the world hates you, keep in mind that it hated me first. ¹⁹ If you belonged to the world, it would love you as its own. As it is, you do not belong to the world, but I have chosen you out of the world. That is why the world hates you. ²⁰ Remember what I told you: 'A servant is not greater than his master.' If they persecuted me, they will persecute you also. If they obeyed my teaching, they will obey yours also.

Jesus, thank You for reminding me that I will be hated.

November 26

Matthew 26:14-16 (NIV)

Judas Agrees to Betray Jesus

[14] Then one of the Twelve—the one called Judas Iscariot—went to the chief priests [15] and asked, "What are you willing to give me if I deliver him over to you?" So they counted out for him thirty pieces of silver. [16] From then on Judas watched for an opportunity to hand him over.

Jesus, no amount of money can cause me to betray You, or so I hope.

ONE DAY MORE THAN WE DESERVE

November 27

Matthew 13:57 (NIV)

⁵⁷ And they took offense at him. But Jesus said to them, "A prophet is not without honor except in his own town and in his own home."

_____

Jesus, I almost know how You feel. It is rough.

PRAYER JOURNAL FOR THE GROWING CHRISTIAN

November 28

Matthew 6:27, 33-34 (NIV)

[27] Can any one of you by worrying add a single hour to your life? [33] But seek first His kingdom and His righteousness, and all these things will be given to you as well. [34] Therefore do not worry about tomorrow, for tomorrow will worry about itself. Each day has enough trouble of its own.

Jesus, thank You for reminding me not to worry.

November 29

Matthew 7:6 (NIV)

⁶"Do not give dogs what is sacred; do not throw your pearls to pigs. If you do, they may trample them under their feet, and turn and tear you to pieces.

Jesus, I will take care of what is important in Your kingdom.

November 30

Matthew 7:8 (NIV)

[8] For everyone who asks receives; the one who seeks finds; and to the one who knocks, the door will be opened.

_____
_____
_____
_____
_____
_____
_____
_____
_____
_____
_____
_____
_____
_____
_____
_____
_____
_____

Thank You, Jesus for Your promises.

… ONE DAY MORE THAN WE DESERVE

Wisdom

Wisdom has nothing to do with age. God grants each of us wisdom according to His will and the fact that we ask. Solomon, the son of David and Bathsheba, was quite wise as gifted by God. Solomon is the author of Proverbs. The first four chapters are about wisdom. The purpose of noting that the four chapters are about wisdom is sharing how important wisdom is.

God places huge importance on wisdom. God considers those of us who do not seek wisdom as foolish. God provides wisdom to us upon request. Wisdom is not something we have to work for or earn. God gives it to us. He just wants us to ask. Likewise, we will be charged with using the wisdom for His glory and for His will. Wisdom will not be used against God's kingdom. That is not in God's will.

Solomon asked for wisdom and he used it to further God's will. Solomon accomplished what David was not able—building a temple and sacrificing to God at a unique level. Further, Solomon understands that wisdom can be shared and not lost. Solomon hopes that we will be wise always. He encourages us to seek wise counsel, not to be wise in our own eyes, and keep focused on the Wisdom Giver!

As we progress in our lives, God will share wisdom in several ways. Our events, circumstances and people will force us to make decisions, changes and alterations which are wiser and less damaging than those same previous decisions would have yielded. Further, God offers wisdom through others, and their influence over us. God can improve your wisdom by simply opening your eyes, ears and hearts. I am always amazed when I meet someone only to realize that I have been in the same space with then but never realized it. It seems to me that God was not ready for me to know that person yet.

As God reveals new information to us, the reveal demonstrates our level of wisdom. Wisdom is not optional, required rather. Wisdom is necessary for the work and will of God. Wisdom dictates our focus on God. Wisdom means knowing when to speak and when to be silent. Wisdom shares knowledge judiciously. Wisdom requires humility and humbleness. Wisdom is present when interacting with people. Wisdom seeks God when confusion, frustration, and strife are present. Wisdom keeps the composure and temper of the person out of trouble. Wisdom embodies difficult decisions.

December 1

Proverbs 4:6 (NIV 1984)

⁶ Do not forsake wisdom, and she will protect you;
love her, and she will watch over you.

_____

God, thank You for the gift of wisdom.

PRAYER JOURNAL FOR THE GROWING CHRISTIAN

December 2

Proverbs 9:8 (NIV 1984)

⁸ Do not rebuke a mocker or he will hate you;
rebuke a wise man and he will love you.

God, help me to discern when to rebuke and who to love.

December 3

Proverbs 10:1 (NIV 1984)

10 The proverbs of Solomon: A wise son brings joy to his father, but a foolish son grief to his mother.

Thank You God for wisdom.

December 4

Proverbs 11:30 (NIV 1984)

[30] The fruit of the righteous is a tree of life, and he who wins souls is wise.

God, I seek to win souls because it is Your will.

December 5

Proverbs 13:20 (NIV 1984)

[20] He who walks with the wise grows wise,
but a companion of fools suffers harm.

God, thank You for those who are wise around me.

PRAYER JOURNAL FOR THE GROWING CHRISTIAN

December 6

Proverbs 3:7 (NIV 1984)

⁷ Do not be wise in your own eyes;
fear the LORD and shun evil.

Lord, help me not to be wise in my own eyes.

ONE DAY MORE THAN WE DESERVE

December 7

Proverbs 17:28 (NIV 1984)

²⁸ Even a fool is thought wise if he keeps silent,
and discerning if he holds his tongue.

Lord, thank You for being able to be quiet at the proper time.

PRAYER JOURNAL FOR THE GROWING CHRISTIAN

December 8

Proverbs 31:26 (NIV 1984)

[26] She speaks with wisdom,
and faithful instruction is on her tongue.

Lord, let me speak with wisdom.

December 9

Daniel 12:3 (NIV 1984)

³ Those who are wise will shine like the brightness of the heavens, and those who lead many to righteousness, like the stars for ever and ever.

Lord, allow me to be wise enough to lead others to righteousness.

December 10

1 Kings 3:12 (NIV1984)

[12] I will do what you have asked. I will give you a wise and discerning heart, so that there will never have been anyone like you, nor will there ever be.

_____
_____
_____
_____
_____
_____
_____
_____
_____
_____
_____
_____
_____
_____
_____
_____
_____

Lord, please give me a wise and discerning heart.

ONE DAY MORE THAN WE DESERVE

December 11

1 Kings 4:29 (NIV1984)

Solomon's Wisdom

[29] God gave Solomon wisdom and very great insight, and a breadth of understanding as measureless as the sand on the seashore.

_____

Lord, give me the type of wisdom which I can use to make a true difference.

December 12

Psalm 19:7 (NIV 1984)

⁷ The law of the LORD is perfect,
reviving the soul.
The statutes of the LORD are trustworthy,
making wise the simple.

___

Lord, thank You for reviving my spirit and being trustworthy.

December 13

Psalm 111:10 (NIV 1984)

¹⁰ The fear of the LORD is the beginning of wisdom;
all who follow his precepts have good understanding.
To him belongs eternal praise.

Lord, I do fear You. I will praise You forever.

December 14

Job 5:13 (NIV 1984)

¹³ He catches the wise in their craftiness,
and the schemes of the wily are swept away.

Lord, thank You for being just.

One Day More Than We Deserve

December 15

1 Corinthians 1:27 (NIV 1984)

²⁷ But God chose the foolish things of the world to shame the wise; God chose the weak things of the world to shame the strong.

Lord, please keep me far away from foolish and weak.

December 16

2 Timothy 3:15 (NIV 1984)

[15] and how from infancy you have known the holy Scriptures, which are able to make you wise for salvation through faith in Christ Jesus.

How long have I known Your word Dear Lord?

December 17

Matthew 11:25 (NIV 1984)

²⁵ At that time Jesus said, "I praise you, Father, Lord of heaven and earth, because you have hidden these things from the wise and learned, and revealed them to little children.

Thank You, Lord, for the gifts You give Your children.

PRAYER JOURNAL FOR THE GROWING CHRISTIAN

December 18

Matthew 11:19 (NIV 1984)

¹⁹ The Son of Man came eating and drinking, and they say, 'Here is a glutton and a drunkard, a friend of tax collectors and "sinners."' But wisdom is proved right by her actions."

Lord, prove the wisdom within me.

December 19

Luke 2:52 (NIV 1984)

⁵² And Jesus grew in wisdom and stature, and in favor with God and men.

Lord, I pray for wisdom and stature.

PRAYER JOURNAL FOR THE GROWING CHRISTIAN

December 20

Romans 11:33 (NIV 1984)

[33] Oh, the depth of the riches of the wisdom and knowledge of God! How unsearchable His judgments, and His paths beyond tracing out!

Lord, I just want to be considered in Your eyes.

December 21

Colossians 2:3 (NIV 1984)

³ in whom are hidden all the treasures of wisdom and knowledge.

Lord, I hope that You have hidden wisdom and treasure within me.

December 22

James 1:5 (NIV 1984)

⁵ If any of you lacks wisdom, he should ask God, who gives generously to all without finding fault, and it will be given to him.

_____
_____
_____
_____
_____
_____
_____
_____
_____
_____
_____
_____
_____
_____
_____
_____
_____
_____
_____
_____

Lord, grant me the wisdom to do Your will. All wisdom.

December 23

1 Kings 4:30 (NIV 1984)

³⁰ Solomon's wisdom was greater than the wisdom of all the men of the East, and greater than all the wisdom of Egypt.

Lord, I am asking for wisdom which leads to leadership of others for Your will to be completed.

December 24

1 Kings 4:34 (NIV 1984)

³⁴ Men of all nations came to listen to Solomon's wisdom, sent by all the kings of the world, who had heard of his wisdom.

_____
_____
_____
_____
_____
_____
_____
_____
_____
_____
_____
_____
_____
_____
_____
_____
_____
_____
_____
_____
_____

Lord, I need wisdom to please You.

One Day More Than We Deserve

December 25

1 Kings 10:24 (NIV 1984)

²⁴ The whole world sought audience with Solomon to hear the wisdom God had put in his heart.

Lord, if You send me, I will go before others and teach Your word, and You will, with the wisdom with which You have granted me.

December 26

Deuteronomy 4:6 (NIV 1984)

⁶ Observe them carefully, for this will show your wisdom and understanding to the nations, who will hear about all these decrees and say, "Surely this great nation is a wise and understanding people."

Lord, surely others will see how You have blessed me with wisdom but only want to please You.

December 27

2 Chronicles 1:10 (NIV 1984)

¹⁰ Give me wisdom and knowledge, that I may lead this people, for who is able to govern this great people of yours?"

_____

Lord, I am requesting knowledge and wisdom to serve You.

December 28

2 Chronicles 1:11-12 (NIV 1984)

[11] God said to Solomon, "Since this is your heart's desire and you have not asked for wealth, riches or honor, nor for the death of your enemies, and since you have not asked for a long life but for wisdom and knowledge to govern my people over whom I have made you king, [12] therefore wisdom and knowledge will be given you. And I will also give you wealth, riches and honor, such as no king who was before you ever had and none after you will have."

Lord, I just want to please and do what is best.

One Day More Than We Deserve

December 29

Proverbs 4:7 (NIV 1984)

The beginning of wisdom is this: Get wisdom. Though it cost all you have, get understanding.

Lord, I seek wisdom and knowledge.

December 30

Job 12:13 (NIV)

¹³ "To God belong wisdom and power; counsel and understanding are His.

Lord, I want wisdom, understanding, counsel, and power because they are Yours and are of You.

December 31

Job 15:8 (NIV)

⁸ Do you listen in on God's council?
Do you have a monopoly on wisdom?

Lord, I just want what You want for me.

Resources

Experiencing God

Disciple's Prayer Life

The Beloved Disciple: A Study of John

Ephesians

David: Seeking a Heart Like His

MasterLife

Abide in Christ

Fellowship with Believers

Live in the Word

Minister to Others

Pray in Faith

Witness to the World

Living God's Word

Hearing God's Voice

When God Speaks

In My Father's House

Esther

PRAYER JOURNAL FOR THE GROWING CHRISTIAN

Acknowledgements

God, thank You for Your plans for me. Thank You for ***One Day More Than We Deserve Daily Devotional and Prayer Journal for Growing Christians*** and choosing me to complete Your project. I just want to please You. Thank You for continuing to anoint me and to invest in me and my gifts, which keep surprising me. Thank You for loving and forgiving me.

Hillary and Nehemiah, thank you for supporting me and my endeavors. Thank you for loving me, especially when I do nothing without a pen and a clipboard, thank you for enduring my late nights, your ideas, the sounding board, the love and the support. Thank you for celebrating our legacy.

To my prayer partners and to my accountability partners, thank you for the long talks and the powerful prayers and the encouragement. To my pastor and church family, thank you so much for your love and support.

Minister Onedia N. Gage seeks to share her study and motivation with you in her outlandish pursuit of God. She hopes that these words bless you. She desires to share her faith in a manner which helps you do the same.

Please feel free to contact and share your testimony. onediagage@onediagage.com or @onediangage (twitter). www.onediagage.com

PRAYER JOURNAL FOR THE GROWING CHRISTIAN

ONE DAY MORE THAN WE DESERVE

PREACHER ♦ ADVOCATE ♦ TEACHER ♦ FACILITATOR

CONFERENCE SPEAKER ♦ WORKSHOP LEADER

To invite Rev. Gage to speak at your church, women's ministry,

Or any other ministry.

Please contact us at: www.onedigage.com

@onediangage (twitter) ♦ onediagage@onediagage.com ♦ facebook.com/onediagageministries

youtube.com/onediagage ♦ blogtalkradio.com/onediagage ♦ ongage (Instagram)

PRAYER JOURNAL FOR THE GROWING CHRISTIAN

ONE DAY MORE THAN WE DESERVE

Publishing

Do you have a book you want to write, but do not know what to do?

Do you have a book you need to publish but do not know how to start?

Would publishing move your career forward?

Let us help

onediagage@purpleink.net ♦ www.purpleink.net

281.740.5143 ♦ 512.715.4243

www.ingramcontent.com/pod-product-compliance
Lightning Source LLC
Chambersburg PA
CBHW031611160426
43196CB00006B/86